American  ~~Common Sense~~

CITIZEN EXPECTATIONS OF OURSELVES

AND OUR GOVERNMENT

Transitioning from
Partisanship and Personality
to Public Policies

Jerry H. Parisella

"Vote Common Sense for Our Common Good"

Dedication

This book is dedicated to three groups of Americans.

First, to those Americans who preceded us, brilliantly forming our nation as a democratic republic in which political power rests with the public through our representatives, determinedly striving to create unity among colonies and states with differing expectations, vigilantly guarding against the dual threats of corruption from within and malign foreign influence from without, astutely engineering, constructing and expanding the infrastructure of a nation, courageously fighting for human freedom, territorial integrity and a rules based world order, boldly reimagining the ideals of what it means to be an American, and ceaselessly advancing the cause of human rights at home and abroad.

Second, to our contemporaries who get up every American morning to do the heavy lifting of making our homes and hospitals, schools and service centers, courts and communication platforms, farms and factories, technologies and transportation modes, recreation centers and retirement homes, every aspect of our communities and national life function as well as our time, talents and treasure allow.

Third, to our future Americans who will face their own opportunities, obstacles, and threats, guided, hopefully, by the accumulated wisdom of those who preceded them, ever mindful of the enduring challenge of Benjamin Franklin, the only person to sign the three key documents in the birth of the United States - the Declaration of Independence on July 4, 1776, the Treaty of Paris ending the Revolutionary War on September 3, 1783, and the Constitution of the United States on September 17, 1787. On the last day of the Constitutional Convention, Mrs. Elizabeth Willing Powel, an influential woman of Philadelphia, asked Franklin, "What have we got a republic or a monarchy?" Benjamin Franklin replied, "A republic if you can keep it."

His challenge is our inheritance for every generation of Americans to preserve and protect.

Acknowledgements

I extend my deepest appreciation to my dear wife who graciously acted as my sounding board, enabling me to bounce ideas off of her and to receive her always insightful feedback.

I also wish to thank my friends who were kind enough to review drafts of the chapters and to provide thoughtful comments and suggestions.

Contents

Introduction

The Bloom Is Off The Rose

When you fly back to the United States from abroad and look out the airplane window, you see the contours of a great land, with rivers winding through miles and miles of forest, wetlands, mountains, and plains as far as the eye can see. As you descend closer to earth, you see the well-laid-out lines of streets, office complexes, industrial areas, and residential communities sprinkled with shopping centers, schools, houses of worship, parks, and parking lots. And just before your plane touches down, you catch a glimpse of ribbons of cars snaking their way over highways and across bridges in a never-ending procession of people going to and fro with appointments to keep, jobs to work, classes to attend, deliveries to make, and friends to visit. It is an impressive sight to behold - that of a country teeming with people, energy, and infrastructure.

But once you are on terra firma, look closer. Some of those cities that look so magnificent from the air contain blighted neighborhoods of closed up shops, abandoned buildings, filthy streets, drug pushers, gun wielding criminals, homeless people, and neglected children. Those office complexes that shine like beacons to capitalism in the night too frequently lay off thousands of people, not as a result of a financial crisis or employee incompetence, but as a matter of normal business practice to quickly cut expenses and boost share price, thereby disrupting the lives of families and wreaking economic havoc on their communities. Those rivers that so beautifully reflect the sun as they effortlessly flow through our cities, towns, and rural areas are all too often unable to sustain their once teeming aquatic life because they flow under the weight of industrial pollutants and agricultural chemicals illegally dumped with disregard for their effect on the environment. Many of the schools to which our children

1

trek each American morning are in deplorable states of disrepair, or are staffed with well-intentioned teachers attempting to stimulate learning without adequate resources. Most horrific of all, schools, offices, shopping malls, theaters, and concert venues are increasingly being turned into killing fields for the slaughtering of innocents through the shocking American phenomenon of frequent mass shootings.

These are the sober realities that reflect sad facts about 21st-century American life. The bloom has come off the American rose.

Since it's founding, America has been considered 'exceptional,' a term first applied to the former British colonies by the French historian Alexis de Tocqueville while travelling here in 1831. Our large land mass size, geography bordered by vast oceans east and west, David vs. Goliath successful revolutionary history, democratic political institutions, laissez-faire inspired economy, rule of law under an independent judiciary, and civil society built upon individual liberties - officially advocated if not consistently practiced - no doubt enabled the United States to develop at unprecedented speed into a global superpower with a quality of life so admired that the country attracted millions of immigrants from around the world, which helped accelerate America's development to a position of economic and military prominence which enabled it to play a decisive role in winning World War II.

America's history is indeed impressive, and its accomplishments, with a few exceptions, are admirable. But, to take a phrase from ancient Greek and Roman societies, we cannot 'rest on our laurels.' We can neither rely upon past achievements and successes, nor fail to adapt to new circumstances and challenges if we wish to sustain the high quality of individual, family, and community life that has characterized the American way of life. As my father used to teasingly ask me as a child, paraphrasing a quote that first appeared in print in an 1862 issue of the Farmers' Almanac,

2

"What is the biggest room in the world? The room for improvement." Indeed, Americans for generations have demonstrated the efficacy of applying this adage, constantly innovating and improving.

At the end of World War II, America took a global leadership role in adopting Secretary of State George Marshall's plan to rebuild the economic infrastructure of the Western European democracies, and in promoting General MacArthur's plan for Japan to transition to democratic self-government, economic stability and peaceful co-existence with other nations. America became the preeminent influencer and facilitator globally. In the following years, our own post-war economy buzzed, housing construction soared, good paying jobs were aplenty, consumer goods were available in abundance, and a spirit of community involvement led to widespread availability of educational, cultural, recreational, religious, and social service resources that enabled generations of Americans to build robust, satisfying lives of purpose and pleasure.

Unfortunately, one unintended consequence of such abundance amidst a much easier life than their elders came naïve assumptions of continuing prosperity without commensurate responsibility. So today, we see that many preventable social problems foolishly go unaddressed, causing needless suffering and harm; growing economic inequality is shrinking the proportion of the population reporting happiness; and we have tragic levels of drug abuse and under-addressed mental health challenges within our population. Moreover, our political system is being undermined by extreme partisanship, public opinion is being compromised by disinformation and disregard of science, and our communities are experiencing greater incivility and eroding public safety.

This begs the question: How is it that a country blessed with tremendous resources, multigenerational innovation, friendly borders, world-class educational, cultural, and religious

3

institutions, cutting edge science, technology, and medicine, highly developed infrastructure and commerce, well equipped law enforcement and a sophisticated legal system, can sustain the levels of selfishness, superficiality, injustice, poverty, abuse, criminality, violence, and mass killings that have become endemic in 21st century American life?

Is this the America that our founders intended? Are we, the current generations of Americans, being good custodians of all that has been entrusted to us to serve future generations? I suspect, indeed hope, that most of us have a gnawing sensation that something is amiss in our country. We need to pay attention to those feelings and respect those thoughts. Our heads are telling us that the incivility, injustice, greed, poverty, crime, violence, eroded sense of community, and political divisiveness that have crept into American life don't belong here, and our hearts are longing for us to craft a better, safer, more civil society for all Americans.

There is an old adage that says, *'Until you acknowledge there is a problem, you can't begin to fix it.'* Similarly, psychology tells us that in order to work on a problem, we must first *'accept'* or *'own'* it. If we acknowledge that these problems are no less aspects of contemporary American life, as are the things about which we are rightly proud about America, then we can have an honest and sensible dialogue about them.

'Honest and sensible,' of course, does not mean launching mean-spirited diatribes, disregarding facts and data, pushing conspiracies, advancing hyper partisanship, or engaging in the type of blame game that too often passes for *'discussion'* in the public space of late. Engaging in recriminations for past injustices, or demonizing those with whom you disagree, is not helpful. What 21st century America needs is for all citizens - together enjoying the rights and benefits of living in this less than perfect but no less great country - to also share in the responsibilities for honestly acknowledging, and collaboratively solving, its problems - our problems. This means that we

Americans must be as quick to embrace our responsibilities to this country as we are to advocate for our rights from this country.

This book is intended to stimulate thoughtful discussions that help transition us from a politics of partisanship and personality toward a politics driven by common sense public policies and responsible personal actions. This book is not is an attempt to be politically correct or to assuage certain group's expectations. Not every reader will agree with everything written, and that's okay. That's the way it should be in a democracy populated by citizens with a diversity of life experiences and expectations.

We can, however, collectively leverage our diversity of life experiences as a strength and embark upon a respectful and determined effort to identify some of our most critical challenges and cooperatively advance common sense solutions to reinvigorate the American way of life - starting with evaluating the substantive policy positions of each politician who seeks our vote.

We are arguably well past the time when we should base our votes upon partisanship or personality, and should now be politically mature enough as an electorate to base our votes upon how sensible are the public policies that a politician will pursue once elected, irrespective of political party. Traditionally liberal or conservative ideologies are no longer able to serve Americans' best interests. What we need now is a transpartisan ideology of common sense that serves the common good.

So, I invite you to join me in looking at just ten critical areas in American society currently begging for common sense solutions from ourselves as citizens and from the politicians in whom we place our trust to run our government. Consider the descriptions of each of the areas challenging us as a country and think about common sense solutions that we should be able to reasonably expect of ourselves and our government.

And feel free to identify what you consider may be additional areas of critical concern.

The suggested solutions herein are just that - suggestions - designed to stimulate discussion among readers and those in our social circles to think about public policies and focus less on the personality or party affiliation of politicians. At the end of each chapter is a brief checklist of points you may wish to consider when you evaluate politicians vying for your vote.

For your convenience, all ten checklists appear together at the end of the book so that you can take copies of the checklists to political events, campaign rallies, candidate debates or whenever watching or listening to politicians speak. Make your own judgments whether a particular candidate - regardless of political affiliation - satisfies you that they will bring to the responsibilities of public office what we should all be able to expect: common sense, compassion, competence, courage, and civility in service of the common good.

What follows is a story that underscores the importance of citizens focusing less on a political personality or party and more on the public policies powering of our democracy.

In 1959, veteran Robert Biggs wrote to Republican president Dwight D. Eisenhower, who had led the Allied forces in Europe during World War II, asking the president to make "direct statements" that would give people the confidence to "back him completely." Americans needed "more of the attitude of a commanding officer who knows the goal and the mission and states, without evasion, the way it is to be done."

Eisenhower answered that "in a democracy, debate is the breath of life. This is to me what Lincoln meant by government 'of the people, by the people, and for the people.'" "Dictatorial systems make one contribution to their people which leads them to tend to support such systems - freedom from the necessity of informing themselves and making up their own minds concerning . . . tremendous complex and difficult questions," Eisenhower wrote.

"But while this responsibility is a taxing one to a free people, it is their great strength as well - from millions of individual free minds come new ideas, new adjustments to emerging problems, and tremendous vigor, vitality, and progress . . . While complete success will always elude us; still it is a quest which is vital to self-government and to our way of life as free men."

This wisdom of former Republican President Dwight D. Eisenhower was echoed years later by former Democratic President John F. Kennedy.

". . . the educated citizen has an obligation to uphold the law. This is the obligation of every citizen in a free and peaceful society – but the educated citizen has a special responsibility by the virtue of his greater understanding. For whether he has ever studied history or current events, ethics or civics, the rules of a profession or the tools of a trade, he knows that only a respect for the law makes it possible for free men to dwell together in peace and progress."

With the wisdom of such leaders inspiring us, let's together think about ten areas of critical concern currently challenging our nation, which resolutions rest in our hands via the politicians whom we place in public office when we step into the voting booth and cast our ballots.

While doing so, let's remember these American mottos:

E Pluribus Unum

This Latin phrase, Out of Many One, has its origins in the idea that from our original thirteen colonies emerged one unified nation. It appears on the great seal of the United States of America.

In God We Trust

This English phrase, in Latin In Deo Speramus, is the official motto of the United States of America. It appears on all the currency of the United States.

Embracing Our Rights and Responsibilities

Striking a Necessary Balance

The First Congress of the United States proposed on September 25, 1789 twelve amendments to our U.S. Constitution, ten of which were ratified by three-quarters of the state legislatures on December 15, 1791. The ratified Articles 3 through 12 constitute the first ten amendments to the Constitution, known as the U.S. Bill of Rights. Over two hundred years after it was proposed, Article 2 was ratified in 1992 as the 27th Amendment to the Constitution. Article 1 was never ratified. From our National Archives, here is a transcription of the 1789 Joint Resolution of Congress Proposing 12 Amendments to the U.S. Constitution:

1789 Joint Resolution of Congress Proposing 12 Amendments to the U.S. Constitution

Congress of the United States began and held at the City of New-York, on Wednesday the fourth of March, one thousand seven hundred and eighty nine.

THE Conventions of a number of the States, having at the time of their adopting the Constitution, expressed a desire, in order to prevent misconstruction or abuse of its powers, that further declaratory and restrictive clauses should be added: And as extending the ground of public confidence in the Government, will best ensure the beneficent ends of its institution.

RESOLVED by the Senate and House of Representatives of the United States of America, in Congress assembled, two thirds of both Houses concurring, that the following Articles be proposed to the Legislatures of the several States, as amendments to the Constitution of the United States, all, or

8

any of which Articles, when ratified by three fourths of the said Legislatures, to be valid to all intents and purposes, as part of the said Constitution; viz.

ARTICLES in addition to, and Amendment of the Constitution of the United States of America, proposed by Congress, and ratified by the Legislatures of the several States, pursuant to the fifth Article of the original Constitution.

Article the first... After the first enumeration required by the first article of the Constitution, there shall be one Representative for every thirty thousand, until the number shall amount to one hundred, after which the proportion shall be so regulated by Congress, that there shall be not less than one hundred Representatives, nor less than one Representative for every forty thousand persons, until the number of Representatives shall amount to two hundred; after which the proportion shall be so regulated by Congress, that there shall not be less than two hundred Representatives, nor more than one Representative for every fifty thousand persons.

Article the second... No law, varying the compensation for the services of the Senators and Representatives, shall take effect, until an election of Representatives shall have intervened.

Article the third... Congress shall make no law respecting an establishment of religion, or prohibiting the free exercise thereof; or abridging the freedom of speech, or of the press; or the right of the people peaceably to assemble, and to petition the Government for a redress of grievances.

Article the fourth... A well regulated Militia, being necessary to the security of a free State, the right of the people to keep and bear Arms, shall not be infringed.

Article the fifth... No Soldier shall, in time of peace, be quartered in any house, without the consent of the Owner, nor in time of war, but in a manner to be prescribed by law.

Article the sixth... The right of the people to be secure in their persons, houses, papers, and effects, against unreasonable searches and seizures, shall not be violated, and no Warrants shall issue, but upon probable cause, supported by Oath or affirmation, and particularly describing the place to be searched, and the persons or things to be seized.

Article the seventh... No person shall be held to answer for a capital, or otherwise infamous crime, unless on a presentment or indictment of a Grand Jury, except in cases arising in the land or naval forces, or in the Militia, when in actual service in time of War or public danger; nor shall any person be subject for the same offence to be twice put in jeopardy of life or limb; nor shall be compelled in any criminal case to be a witness against himself, nor be deprived of life, liberty, or property, without due process of law; nor shall private property be taken for public use, without just compensation.

Article the eighth... In all criminal prosecutions, the accused shall enjoy the right to a speedy and public trial, by an impartial jury of the State and district wherein the crime shall have been committed, which district shall have been previously ascertained by law, and to be informed of the nature and cause of the accusation; to be confronted with the witnesses against him; to have compulsory process for obtaining witnesses in his favor, and to have the Assistance of Counsel for his defence.

Article the ninth... In suits at common law, where the value in controversy shall exceed twenty dollars, the right of trial by jury shall be preserved, and no fact tried by a jury, shall be otherwise re-examined in any Court of the United States, than according to the rules of the common law.

Article the tenth... Excessive bail shall not be required, nor excessive fines imposed, nor cruel and unusual punishments inflicted.

Article the eleventh... The enumeration in the Constitution, of certain rights, shall not be construed to deny or disparage others retained by the people.

Article the twelfth... The powers not delegated to the United States by the Constitution, nor prohibited by it to the States, are reserved to the States respectively, or to the people.

Absent such brilliant initiatives of our Founding Fathers in creating the U.S. Constitution and Bill Of Rights, we would not have the rights and liberties that we have enjoyed for generations and which many people tend to take for granted. For most of recorded history, humans have lived as 'subjects' of monarchies and oligarchies, or of dictators, or as 'citizens' in name only subject to the whims of theocracies, communism, or other forms of oppressive governance and control. Even now, in the twenty-first century, we still see many countries around the globe organized and operated under soul-suppressing forms of government control. According to The Economist Democracy Index: only 8.0% of the world's population live in 24 authentic democracies; 37.3% of the world's population live in 48 flawed democracies; 17.9% of the world's population live under 36 hybrid regimes; and 36.8% of the world's population live under 59 authoritarian regimes. The United States and other freedom loving democracies are a minority - a very fortunate minority.

As a constitutional, representative democracy, the United States vests power in the people and the states in which they live and spells that out in a written governing constitution, which provides that the citizens elect their representatives to represent their concerns and desires within government. This enables the free expression of the will of the people and well respects human rights and personal liberties.

We Americans rightly exercise our freedoms and claim our rights without hesitation, as well as we should. What we don't do as readily is take on our citizen responsibilities, which are of no less importance in sustaining our civil society. With rights

11

come responsibilities and while the former get plenty of expression and attention, the latter tend to get overlooked and neglected. This represents a challenge to all of us to strike a better balance in order that our constitutional democracy sustains a civil society in which everyone can live freely and without fear.

At the founding of our country, personal character was largely shaped by the moral and religious teachings of the Bible. In 1780, the Constitution of the Commonwealth of Massachusetts, largely the work product of John Adams, Samuel Adams, and James Bowdoin, and the oldest written constitution still in effect, had a focus on moral and character development and provided the foundation for the public school system which was expected to develop in students the habits required for democratic citizenship. Here are two illustrative sections:

1780 Constitution of the Commonwealth of Massachusetts

PART THE FIRST

Art. III. As the happiness of a people and the good order and preservation of civil government essentially depend upon piety, religion, and morality, and as these cannot be generally diffused through a community but by the institution of the public worship of God and of the public instructions in piety, religion, and morality: Therefore, To promote their happiness and to secure the good order and preservation of their government, the people of this commonwealth have a right to invest their legislature with power to authorize and require, and the legislature shall, from time to time, authorize and require, the several towns, parishes, precincts, and other bodies-politic or religious societies to make suitable provision, at their own expense, for the institution of the public worship of God and for the support and maintenance of public Protestant teachers of piety, religion, and morality in all cases where such provision shall not be made voluntarily.

CHAPTER V.

Section 2.--The Encouragement of Literature, etc.

Wisdom and knowledge, as well as virtue, diffused generally among the body of the people, being necessary for the preservation of their rights and liberties; and as these depend on spreading the opportunities and advantages of education in the various parts of the country, and among the different orders of the people, it shall be the duty of legislatures and magistrates, in all future periods of this commonwealth, to cherish the interests of literature and the sciences, and all seminaries of them; especially the university at Cambridge, public schools, and grammar-schools in the towns; to encourage private societies and public institutions, rewards and immunities, for the promotion of agriculture, arts, sciences, commerce, trades, manufactures, and a natural history of the country; to countenance and inculcate the principles of humanity and general benevolence, public and private charity, industry and frugality, honesty and punctuality in their dealings; sincerity, and good humor, and all social affections and generous sentiments, among the people.

Thomas Jefferson, (1743-1826), our third President, was also a proponent of moral education in our schools, believing that it was important for youth to practice virtuous behavior and love for their country. Among his wisest quotes was, *"Educate and inform the whole mass of people. They are the only sure reliance for the preservation of our liberty."*

Horace Mann, (1796-1859), considered the father of American public education, had one of the most significant influences on character development. He was more concerned with youth acquiring moral reasoning through instruction rather than factual academic instruction. *"The mind(s) and heart(s) of students should be open to, and closely monitored by, the teacher so that*

13

character education could be accomplished in a timely and responsible manner."

William Homes McGuffey, (1800-1873), educator and author, also had a significant influence in American character education. His series of textbooks, the 'McGuffey Readers,' were designed to help students read and introduced character development in patriotism, good citizenship, and morality.

Starting around the 1890s, as the United States increasingly industrialized, a different posture toward education emerged that emphasized academics and standards and gave less attention to moral instruction. Over time, and with demographic changes, the development of teacher unions, and the adoption of academic testing, the education experience of students underwent significant change. After World War II, education was more oriented toward academic competence rather than moral training. And presumably due to misunderstandings about the separation of church and state, American society veered away from the historical and philosophical ideas that had shaped young minds and moved toward principles of behaviorism, the theory that human behavior is best explained by conditioning, rather than appealing to thoughts and feelings. The cumulative effect was that the majority of teachers stopped teaching moral education.

From the onset of the Cold War, demand for academic and cognitive excellence surpassed that for moral, civic, and social education. Moreover, disagreements about what should be taught in classrooms regarding values and morals effectively shifted responsibility for values and morals education from the school to families and religious organizations. By the late 1960s, character development had largely faded as a goal of public education. Not surprisingly, this had unintended consequences for our society.

There is no question that academic instruction, talent development, measuring achievement and experiential opportunities are all important. But absent moral values to

14

shape thinking and guide behaviors, we tend to end up with more selfish citizens, smarter criminals and an increasingly uncivil society. Character matters so much so that the absence of certain values among many has become painfully obvious in current society.

As we look at today's state of affairs in America, too many able-bodied citizens lack a strong work ethic and instead primarily look to government welfare benefits, or resort to scams and illegal activities to make money. Far too many drivers on the road show a wanton disregard for public safety, endangering themselves and their fellow citizens by driving recklessly, disobeying traffic signals, or driving under the influence of alcohol or drugs. Social media is being exploited to taunt people to engage in dangerous and illegal activities, such as subway surfing, fraud, spreading conspiracies, and issuing death threats. The convenience of online retailing is being subverted by some to sell ill-gotten goods, stimulating smash-and-grab retail theft in brick-and-mortar stores, which is costing businesses money and inconveniencing shoppers with more items under lock-and-key.

Citizens who do not exercise self-discipline against engaging in negative behavior force society to hire more police and parole officers, increase court capacity, and build more prisons to incarcerate more criminals. But there is a limit to how widespread and robust a law enforcement infrastructure we can afford. And who wants to live in a police state?

The widespread emergence of negative behaviors are a reflection of our failure to shape the character of younger generations, made even more difficult by the decline in participation in houses of worship, scouting organizations, philosophy classes, and other traditional sources that once conveyed good moral values from one generation to the next. What is more recently filling the vacuum is the content being fed to people on the internet, including social media platforms which disseminate text and imagery that undermine human

15

dignity, attack self-esteem, distort reality, spread disinformation, set unreal expectations, promote sexual obsessions, diminish real-world human connections and glorify violence.

Young people are being hit with the doubly destructive dose of adults' failure to inculcate good moral values and the associated self-respect, mutual respect, and sound judgment that accompany those values, and of being exposed to hours and hours of largely unregulated, mind-numbing online content that works against good character development. In short, the good values and morals that our elders wisely passed onto us and which helped shape and secure our civil society are not being as widely or robustly passed on to many younger generations of Americans, denying them essential ingredients to build lives of purpose and meaning and effectively undermining the foundations of our civil society. And it is not the fault of young people. Responsibility rests squarely with many adults who should know better, but who have let such an unhealthy and unhelpful environment emerge thanks to the greed of some and the neglect of many.

Numerous studies have demonstrated that children learn moral values and behaviors by observing their parents or closest relatives. Kids tend to internalize and imitate those adult behaviors. If their closest adults don't demonstrate respect, fairness, and compassion in dealing with others, what can we expect of these children's behavior? If the adults in their lives don't live with a strong work ethic, honesty and personal financial responsibility, how can we expect the children to grow up and live that way? If the adults abuse family members or themselves, engage in illegal activities, primarily look to welfare rather than to work in order to support themselves, engage in promiscuity, and thumb their noses at society's norms, we shouldn't be surprised when their children replicate those behaviors when they become adults.

Historically, across the globe the family has been the primary vehicle to instill moral values and build personal character in children. But for far too many families, they are unable to serve that critical role. Almost 90% of the world's population now live in countries with falling marriage rates. In the United States, marriage has declined by 60% since the 1970s, largely due to rising divorce rates, an increase in women's educational attainment and labor force participation, and the growing popularity of cohabitating without the benefit of a marital commitment. And of those who do marry, half of first marriages end in divorce, and an even higher percentage of multiple marriages fail.

African Americans have become the most unmarried, with more than two out of three black women unmarried. They are more than twice as likely as white women to never marry. One reason that marriage has declined within the African American community is that black women have advanced economically and educationally, but black men have fallen behind. Nearly twice as many black women graduate from college annually than black men.

About 40% of births in the United States occur outside of marriage, up from 28% in the 1990s. Half of non-marital births are to non-cohabitating couples. Even among the other half of non-marital births that do occur with cohabitating couples, these relationships tend to be less stable and have fewer economic resources compared to married couples. The absence of married parents risks emotional and behavioral problems for their children.

These trends are deeply concerning because marriage is associated with many benefits for individuals and families, including better health, longevity, and higher income. Declining marriage rates put more children at risk of growing up poor, which can impact their health and future economic prospects. And in the absence of acquiring good moral values from their closest adults, they are at increased risk of engaging in harmful, self-destructive, illegal, even criminal behavior. No one wins. The children are short changed, their negative behavior undermines safety and civility in our communities, and our law enforcement and judicial systems become over burdened - to the point in some states that quite a number of crimes no longer lead to arrest or behavior-changing meaningful accountability, the absence of which has the unintended effect of providing a perverse incentive to continue to engage in serial criminal activity. Families and their power to inculcate good moral values matter, but both are weakening in our society.

Most Americans would agree that each citizen can, indeed, should play a positive role in sustaining self and society. But what exactly does that mean? If we look historically, a good foundation to answering that question was laid in 1910 with the inception of the Boy Scouts of America (BSA) in which programs have participated more than 130 million youngsters, thanks to the 35 million adult volunteers who have helped to carry out the BSA's mission to prepare young people to make ethical and moral choices over their lifetimes by instilling in them the values of the Scout Oath and Scout Law:

SCOUT OATH: On my honor, I will do my best to do my duty to God and my country and to obey the Scout Law; to help other people at all times; to keep myself physically strong, mentally awake, and morally straight.

SCOUT LAW: A Scout is trustworthy, loyal, helpful, friendly, courteous, kind, obedient, cheerful, thrifty, brave, clean and reverent.

For multiple generations, the experience of scouting programs allowed young people to try new and fun things, provide service to others, build self-confidence, and acquire ethical standards, thereby facilitating American youth on a path toward contributing to a more conscientious, responsible, and productive society. Sadly, the Boy Scouts of America, as well as the Girl Scouts of the USA, have experienced tremendous declines in participation for decades, with the former exacerbated by financial stress and reputational damage from thousands of molestation lawsuits.

If we look to the U.S. military and the particular values of each of the Services, we find enduring values that have influenced generations. The Department of Defense values leadership, professionalism, and technical know-how, as well as duty, integrity, ethics, honor, courage, and loyalty. Each Service has its own defined core values. The values of the Air Force, in which I served as a young man: integrity first, service before self, and excellence in all we do. For those who served in the Army: loyalty, duty, respect, selfless service, honor, integrity, and personal courage. For the Navy and Marines: honor, courage, and commitment. And for those who served in the Coast Guard: honor, respect, and devotion to duty.

Although these core values were developed for military service, any American citizen would do well to embrace them. Who can argue against any of these values? Imagine if every American lived these values. Wouldn't we have less domestic violence and sexual abuse, reduced levels of crime, safer streets and highways, fewer scams and cases of fraud, less tax evasion, fewer mass shootings, etc.? Of course, we would, and not only would the quality of people's lives in America significantly rise, but our expenditure of citizen tax monies to ameliorate all of those social ills would substantially decline. A win-win situation if there ever was one.

Unfortunately, there are fewer and fewer Americans being exposed to those values in military service, thereby undermining the role model ripple effects in their communities. Since 1987, active duty military service has declined by 39%. In a 2022 survey of people ages 16 to 24 asking about their likelihood to join the military, 32% reported 'probably not,' and 58% reported 'definitely not,' amounting to 90%. Among the top reasons reported, were possibility of physical or emotional injury, leaving family and friends, other career interests, and dislike of military lifestyle.

That decline parallels lower levels of civilian volunteerism, something that has been part of American life since Benjamin

Franklin encouraged his fellow Philadelphians to establish our first volunteer firefighting brigade in 1736, the Union Fire Company. According to AmeriCorps, the federal agency for national service and volunteerism, formal volunteer participation in America fell to 23.2% between 2019 and 2021, a 7% decline that is the largest drop since tracking began in 2002. As many in the field note, volunteering is the glue that keeps the community working. When fewer people engage with each other, it results in reduced levels of trust in one other and greater social isolation.

Unfortunately, with fewer people serving in military service and thinner ranks in civilian volunteer organizations, our society is left with weaker nationally shared platforms for character development and public service. What is happening simultaneously is that young people especially are being influenced by a dizzying array of content on the internet, which is pushed with little concern for its impact on their self-esteem and character development and which promotes a false sense of community with the artificiality of virtual connections.

Into the breach, we would be well advised to consider how to reinvigorate our culture with the moral values which enhance human dignity, civility, and community. One idea that comes to mind: develop a teaching curriculum, and a reinforcing public service advertising campaign, designed around six personal responsibilities and an equal number of civic responsibilities. The following suggested responsibilities are not intended to be exhaustive but to stimulate discussion within American families and communities about how we can better serve our youth and inspire our adults, thereby enhancing the quality of American life for all citizens.

Six Personal Responsibilities

BE A PERSON OF GOOD CHARACTER, someone who is honest in word and deed. Let your 'yes' be yes and your 'no' be no. Be truthful with your words, authentic in your relationships, and honest with your transactions. Do the right thing even when no one notices simply because it's the right thing to do.

BE A PERSON OF COMPASSION, someone who empathizes with those who experience suffering. If it's within your power to relieve suffering, to lighten someone's load, or to encourage and support, do it without expecting anything in return. Wouldn't you want to be treated with compassion?

BE A PERSON OF INTEGRITY, someone whom others can trust. When you make a commitment to do something, do it so that you earn your own respect and can be relied upon by the people in your life.

BE A PERSON WITH PURPOSE AND PERSISTENCE, someone who uses your time, talent, and treasure for good of self and of others and who perseveres in the face of the inevitable obstacles and setbacks of life. As Albert Einstein famously remarked, *"Genus is 1% talent and 99% hard work."* Pursue your purpose with passion and perseverance.

BE A SENSIBLE PERSON, someone who exercises common sense, thinks logically, differentiates facts from fiction, and forms opinions based upon data, not hearsay. In this regard, school curricula could include more coursework around research and critical thinking.

BE A PERSON OF SELF-RESPECT AND MUTUAL RESPECT. Be honest with yourself and treat yourself with equal measures of kindness and self-discipline. Engage in difficult conversations with respect, rationality, empathy, and patience. Treat others the way that you want to be treated.

Six Civic Responsibilities

BE A CITIZEN WHO RESPECTS THE LIVES AND INTERESTS OF YOUR FELLOW CITIZENS, no matter how different they may be in appearance, origin, creed, lifestyle, or opinions. We are not required to like everyone nor to agree with everyone's decisions or lifestyles, but in a civil, democratic, diverse society, we do have to respect everyone and, at times, notwithstanding some reluctance, to accept differences.

BE A CITIZEN WHO OBEYS THE LAWS of the city, county, state, and nation in which you live, whether it applies to attending school, paying taxes, being licensed for particular activities, obeying traffic regulations, owning a weapon, serving on a jury, participating in a government census, etc. This is certainly not asking too much to enjoy the benefits of our free society.

BE A CITIZEN WHO VOLUNTEERS FOR PUBLIC SERVICE, whether in any branches of the military or Coast Guard, or in a civilian organization, perhaps assisting the handicapped, visiting the homebound, coaching young athletes, teaching English to immigrants, distributing food and clothing to the poor, helping at an animal shelter, etc.

BE A CITIZEN WHO STAYS INFORMED about local, national and global affairs by regularly accessing accurate information reported by trained journalists through credible news organizations and use that information to form fact and data-based opinions. And apply your God-given rationality, and God-expected commitment to truth, to differentiate fact from fiction and embrace the former irrespective of how attractive or popular may be the latter.

BE A CITIZEN WHO EXERCISES THE HARD WON RIGHT TO VOTE for our elected representatives based upon an accurate understanding of each politician's character and public policy positions. And if you have the talents and skills, consider working for a government agency or running for public office. Positions in public service, whether competitively earned, appointed or elected, contribute to sustaining healthy communities, defending civil society, and advancing our constitutional democracy toward its multigenerational goal of a more perfect union.

BE A CITIZEN WHO TREATS YOUR NEIGHBORS POLITELY, who helps others without being asked, who calls out injustice when encountered, who leads by example and who inspires others to be nicer and to do better. The worst that can happen is that more people might respect you, like you, and be more inclined to help you when you need it.

These six personal and six civic responsibilities don't seem like such a heavy lift, yet they could transform our society, eradicating some of its shortcomings and enhancing some of its potential. In considering citizen rights and responsibilities, consider the words of our 35th President, John F. Kennedy, spoken on January 20, 1961 during his inaugural address, "*And so, my fellow Americans: Ask not what your country can do for you; ask what you can do for your country.*" Bigger picture, he continued, addressing the international audience, "*My fellow citizens of the world: ask not what America will do for you, but what together we can do for the freedom of man.*"

What We Can Do

It is incumbent upon all citizens to become informed about the critical issues facing our nation and our communities. With our rights come responsibilities, not the least of which is making informed choices at the ballot box. To help in this regard, below is a Candidate Evaluation checklist which you can use to evaluate politicians campaigning for your vote to hold public office. Assess them yourself and decide which candidate is best prepared and most likely to take a transpartisan common sense approach to advancing citizen rights and responsibilities.

23

Candidate Evaluation Criteria

	Candidate _____'s Position on Citizen Rights and Responsibilities	Yes/No
1	Advocates adding moral values teaching and critical thinking to high school curricula	
2	Sponsors tuition and tax incentives to encourage public and military service	
3	Strengthens oversight of tech companies to limit harmful content and illegal activity	
4	Creates public service advertising campaigns that teach personal and civic responsibilities	
5	Requires formal orientation of immigrants to expected personal and civic responsibilities	
6	As a public official, models those personal and civic responsibilities.	

The information, data and statistics mentioned came from a wide variety of open sources available over the internet. A debt of gratitude is expressed for the hard work of all those people at so many different private and public sector organizations who spend countless hours collecting and collating data, researching information, verifying facts, and producing reports for public consumption, which profoundly facilitates the creation of an informed citizenry upon which our democracy depends. Among those sources:

Library of Congress

Sutori.com

ThePublicDiscourse.com

Time Magazine

Journal of Education

TimeToast.com

USscouts.org

Department of Defense

Americorps

The Economist Democracy Index

Wikipedia

Stanford University Center of Comparative Studies

Population Reference Bureau

PewResearch.org

USAfacts.org

ScienceDirect.org

Statista.com

UN.org

Census.gov

OECD.org

Wikipedia

WorldBank.org

Respecting the Dignity of Workers

Together Co-Creating the American Way of Life

Work, the intentional effort to produce or accomplish something, is essential to human nature, baked into our DNA. We learn this in the first pages of the Bible where we see that, when God created humans, He put them in the Garden of Eden to cultivate and care for it - to labor. Work was not a punishment but a gift that enables humans to utilize their talents and energy to harness the forces of nature for the development of the human community. God gave to humans the awesome power to be co-creators, to develop the earth into an environment where humans, animals, and all life forms can thrive and glorify God.

Admittedly, it is difficult to conceive of work in such a positive and inspiring way when what many experience in this post-industrial, technological age is demoralizing drudgery and disheartening disrespect that can damage our self-esteem, diminish our health, disrupt family life, and disturb our sense of peace. Work during our mortal lives may never be as beautiful an experience as that envisioned in the Garden of Eden, but work can certainly be organized in much better ways than current practices in order to better affirm human dignity.

Imagine if work was the environment in which we could grow as humans, exercising our creativity, expanding our knowledge, developing our talents, fostering collaborative relationships, growing organizations that reflect our values, and producing profits that are equitably shared among all stakeholders, including workers, investors and providers of public services.

To a large extent, capitalism has already laid the groundwork for such a productive environment. History has shown that no other form of economic organization has

26

proven to be as efficient as capitalism in encouraging creativity, allocating capital, balancing supply-and-demand, rewarding effort, and creating wealth. But while creating all of these societal goods, capitalism has also created harm, including slavery, child labor, unsafe work environments, excessively long work schedules, discrimination, unfair wages, and environmental degradation, to name a few. Capitalism, left to its own devices, pursues profits irrespective of the harm caused to others - to workers, families, communities, the environment, et al. That's not to say that capitalism is bad; it's only to acknowledge that capitalism is simply a form of economic organization that needs to be thoughtfully encouraged and sensibly regulated to ensure that it maximizes good and minimizes harm.

Thankfully, we have a legacy of trying to do just that. Here are seven American examples of how creating a sensible regulatory environment within which capitalism operates has respected the dignity of workers and increased the wellbeing of their families.

Standard Five Day Work Week (1929)

This was the revolutionary proposal put forward by the Amalgamated Clothing Workers of America in 1929. This union was the first to ever demand a five-day workweek and receive it. After that, the rest of the country fell quickly into line, and the five-day workweek became the standard. Can you imagine life now without two-day weekends?

Social Security Act (1935)

This New Deal legislation, signed into law by President Roosevelt, provided workers with unemployment insurance, aid to dependent children, and rehabilitation for the physically disabled. It also improved public health and provided pensions to workers in their old age. How many of our elderly and disabled would have lived lives in complete impoverishment without this once radical proposal?

27

Fair Labor Standards Act (1938)

The FLSA, also signed into law by President Roosevelt, granted sweeping protections to workers — establishing a minimum wage and the 8-hour work day, providing for overtime, and prohibiting the use of child labor in all businesses engaged in interstate commerce. These were once controversial ideas that today we can't imagine doing without.

Civil Rights Act / Title VII (1964)

This landmark legislation, proposed by President Kennedy and signed into law by President Johnson, prohibited discrimination in public places, provided for the integration of schools and public facilities, and made employment discrimination illegal. Title VII of the Act created the Equal Employment Opportunity Commission to implement and enforce the laws that prohibit discrimination based on race, color, religion, sex, national origin, disability, or age in hiring, promoting, firing, setting wages, testing, training, apprenticeship and all other terms and conditions of employment.

Occupational Safety & Health Act (1970)

Providing a safe workplace had been a primary goal of the labor movement since its inception. Many years later, President Nixon was convinced to sign the first comprehensive federal legislation covering safety in the workplace. This landmark legislation has reduced countless workplace injuries, illnesses, and fatalities among American workers.

Employee Retirement Income Security Act (1974)

ERISA, signed into law by President Ford, ensures minimum standards for the majority of private industry pension and health plans, as well as other benefit plans such as life insurance. Among its requirements is that employees must be notified of benefit plan terms, including coverage, costs, and funding. And it ushered in Individual Retirement Accounts to give individuals not covered by retirement plans at work a tax-advantaged savings plan, which allows the rollover of assets with job changes and at retirement.

Family and Medical Leave Act (1993)

FMLA, signed into law by President Clinton, requires organizations with 50 or more employees to provide employees who have worked at least 1,250 hours over the past 12 months with up to 12 work weeks of job-protected unpaid leave during any 12 months to recover from a serious illness or to care for a new child or a seriously ill family member.

These are just seven examples that demonstrate that slowly but surely, over time, and often in the face of stiff resistance, we enhance the regulatory framework within which we expect organizations to operate. And we do this not just to protect workers but also, among other things, to promote fair competition, disclose truthful product information to consumers, reduce damage to the environment, and ensure that corporations, no less than citizens, pay their fair share of taxes to support society's institutions and the infrastructure upon which we all depend in order for people to live their lives and for organizations to conduct their activities.

Businesses don't operate in a vacuum. They have offices, research facilities, call centers, manufacturing sites, distribution hubs, etc., within communities upon which they depend for everything - from workers who were educated in local schools to electrical power, water, and sanitation services to run their facilities, to a transportation infrastructure over which to distribute their goods, to a court system to adjudicate commercial disputes, to police and fire departments to respond to emergencies - the list could go on and on. Businesses and communities thrive through this symbiotic relationship.

And just as businesses depend upon the communities in which they operate, workers depend upon businesses to provide them with opportunities to utilize their talents, to earn a living wage to support themselves and their families, to develop confidence that they are contributing to their community, to plan and save for future needs, to pay their fair share of taxes and to contribute to private pensions and public social security so that they will have adequate monthly income to meet their living expenses when they become too old or disabled to work. The triangular relationship among society, business, and workers is mutually beneficial, though we frequently err in putting the interests of business ahead of those of society and workers. And occasionally, workers may overreach with unrealistic expectations of business or society.

A great deal of attention is given to protecting financial capital and much less to protecting human capital, in spite of the reality that people are the source and the goal of all economic activity. People ideate the concepts that give rise to products around which businesses are built. People marshal the tools, whether manual, automated, or computer-generated, to build the products and provide the services upon which people depend. And people are the stewards of the financial capital, which provides the transactional fuel to power these activities. People should be recognized as the end-all and be all of our economic activities.

Of notable importance, those tasked with managing human and financial capital are expected to do so with competence, integrity, and fairness in order that organizations succeed and fulfill society's needs, doing so honestly, profitably and equitably. Competent coordination of both human and financial capital can yield mutually beneficial economic benefits for many generations, while incompetent, inequitable, or dishonest management can lead to the ruination of organizations, the disruption of lives, and the diminishment of communities.

We have plenty of business schools, sophisticated corporations, and savvy market investors who adeptly apply their expertise to the astute allocation of financial capital and management of risks and returns. And our capitalist society unhesitatingly bestows attention and kudos on those who amass wealth and show off their luxurious lifestyles and, for some, their generosity.

What we have much less of is interest in and expertise around ensuring that workers are given equal consideration in the calculus of running for-profit businesses. Even less attention is given to the millions of hard-working Americans who do the heavy lifting every day to keep the non-commercial organizations in our society functioning, from hospitals to government agencies to charitable organizations, etc., yet rarely get the recognition that they deserve. This needs to change.

The recent, once in a century pandemic reminded us, ever so briefly, of our dependence upon healthcare workers who took care of the sick and dying amid a circulating deadly virus, in spite of the risks to themselves. When police officers or firefighters die in the performance of their duties, we pay them our respect. And the folks who provide personal services typically receive tips for good service or at the holidays. But that's about it for recognition, and it's woefully inadequate considering that society could not function - and shareholders could not make their profits and capital gains - if we didn't have so many people performing so much work, day in and day out, sadly with little recognition for their efforts.

I invite you to take a few moments to think imaginatively about these admittedly unlikely possible scenarios and ask yourself, how could our society function...

if we didn't have teachers to educate our children, custodians to keep classrooms clean, groundskeepers to keep playing fields groomed, engineers to maintain school heating and ventilation systems, bus drivers to transport children safely, et al?

if we didn't have police officers to catch criminals, firefighters to fight fires, emergency medical technicians to

31

respond to health crises, corrections officers to keep criminals away from law abiding citizens, district attorneys to prosecute criminals, and public defenders to protect the innocent, et al.?

if we didn't have harbor masters to direct cargo ships into our ports, longshoremen to unload the goods upon which we depend, air traffic controllers to safely guide aircraft in and out of our airports, flight and ground crews to fly and service the planes on which we travel, train and track crews to enable subways and trains to bring us to our desired destinations, delivery service drivers to bring us the multitude of goods that we order every day, et al.?

if we didn't have architects, engineers, constructors, electricians, plumbers, carpenters, other craftsmen, and laborers to construct the factories and buildings in which we work and the homes in which we live?

if we didn't have farmers, laborers, food inspectors, truck drivers, grocery cashiers, cooks, kitchen staff, bartenders, baristas, waiters and waitresses, et al., to keep us fed and hydrated?

if we didn't have workers to plow our streets of snow, clear our sidewalks of trash, repair the potholes in our roads, trim the trees encroaching on power lines, tow our disabled vehicles, et al.

if we didn't have engineers, energy producers, power distributors, network managers, telecommunications specialists, cable layers, line workers, web developers, software writers, help desk agents, cyber security analysts, et al. to power our personal, business, and governmental activities and to facilitate our telephone calls, internet activities and home entertainment?

if we didn't have doctors, nurses, dentists, respiratory therapists, x-ray technicians, optometrists, pharmacists, chiropractors, physical therapists, assisted living staff, et al. looking after our health?

if we didn't have psychiatrists, psychologists, therapists, counselors, priests, pastors, rabbis, imams, et al. to help with our mental, emotional, and spiritual well-being?

if we didn't have veterinarians, technicians, animal shelter staff, pet food suppliers, dog walkers, adoption agency workers, et al, to provide care for our beloved pets?

if we didn't have hair dressers, barbers, manicurists, homecare attendants, launderers, cleaners, gardeners, appliance repairers, maintenance contractors, doormen, porters, et al. upon whom we depend for a myriad of necessary services?

if we didn't have government employees like military service members, CIA analysts, FBI agents, CDC scientists, DOT investigators, environmental engineers, social workers, election workers, county administrators, town clerks, et al., upon whom we depend for a safe, stable, and sustainable society?

These are just a few of the 157 million often over looked American workers upon whom we all depend - rich and poor alike - to keep our country functioning in order that we can live our lives as best we can, and without which life as we know it would come to a screeching halt. We occasionally get a whiff of what that might be like when a group of organized workers is unable to negotiate a satisfactory agreement with their employer and resort to a strike to pressure interested parties to reach an agreement. It's one thing to have delays at an airport, fewer automobiles coming off an assembly line, a brief suspension of elective procedures at a hospital, or a temporary postponement of school classes. These events, thankfully, happen only occasionally and rarely simultaneously. But imagine the unimaginable if all workers across our entire society just stopped doing their jobs all at the same time. The American way of life would cease to exist.

That's not going to happen, of course, but just the thought of it can serve as a mental catalyst to prompt all of us to develop a greater appreciation for our fellow citizens upon whom we all depend, the men and women who do the heavy lifting each day and who for too long have been taken for granted. And with that greater appreciation should come the motivation for us to take another step forward in further enhancing the dignity of American workers.

In this regard, four areas for improvement come to mind: (1) reversing the off-shoring of American jobs and dependence upon foreign suppliers; (2) wisely managing automation and artificial intelligence; (3) expanding defined benefit pensions and Social Security funding; and (4) honoring monthly the contribution of various categories of American workers.

REVERSING THE OFF-SHORING OF AMERICAN JOBS AND DEPENDENCE UPON FOREIGN SUPPLIERS

In the course of businesses trying to lower their costs-of-goods sold, some have sought to move production out of the United States, where they enjoyed their first measures of success, to other countries where workers are paid less for their labor, or energy is cheaper, or taxes are lower, or environmental regulations are looser, etc. Pretty much anything that increases a company's profit margins is usually welcomed by the shareholders of those companies. Unfortunately, American workers suffer the brunt of these off-shoring decisions in lost jobs and incomes upon which they and their families depend. And the burden of these business decisions is not limited to just the former employees. The communities in which they live also suffer the loss of local jobs, income, and tax revenue - from the small local businesses where those workers used to spend their money, to the schools and libraries which have fewer resources to fund their activities, to entire regions of a state when an industry shuts down operations here and starts them in another country.

Not only is the financial impact harmful, but the psychic cost to the workers, particularly those unable to access retraining resources and get other comparably compensated

34

jobs, is no less devastating. Their sense of self-esteem in being productive, contributing to their community and supporting themselves and their families are all threatened. Particularly in a one industry town, when that industry shuts its doors and moves elsewhere, those left behind with few alternatives endure such levels of anxiety and stress that some fall into depression, resort to abuse of alcohol or drugs, or take their frustrations out through emotional or physical abuse.

The corporations and their shareholders enjoy the benefits of these off-shoring decisions with little obligation to their former workers, or to the communities whose public infrastructure enabled the corporations to originally launch, grow, scale, and expand their operations. Some corporations may offer one-time severance payments or retraining programs, but the payments typically are quite modest and the retraining programs are often of limited benefit, especially if there aren't other organizations nearby to employ the displaced workers.

Another huge and unforeseen harm from these decisions to go offshore has been the development of dangerous dependence upon foreign manufacturing and associated vulnerability to supply chain disruptions. The recent pandemic dramatically brought these issues home to Americans when it became painfully obvious that we didn't have enough supply of some of the most basic goods for healthcare and personal care, when automobile manufacturing slowed because of depleted inventories of foreign manufactured computer chips, and when consumer product shortages led to empty shelves and artificially inflated prices which hurt many families' budgets. It took a once in a century pandemic to finally realize that even our national security was compromised by some corporations having moved to foreign countries the production of certain component parts upon which our military depends to maintain its equipment in a constant state of readiness.

If the degradation of formerly vibrant industrial areas into 'rust belts' didn't awaken us to the dangers of shuttering operations here and moving productive capacity to other countries, then the pandemic certainly should have. We need to learn from this experience and develop new industrial and commercial policies to ensure that corporations return and retain significant domestic production capacity for products and parts upon which we have a critical dependence. That will strengthen our nation's security, enhance our preparedness for future unexpected calamities, create more jobs, increase the tax base for communities, and enable workers to better plan for their families' financial futures.

Some corporations have already begun to do just that. They should be applauded for doing so and offered as examples to encourage resistant corporations to follow suit voluntarily. If they do not, then in critical industries, it is not unreasonable for government to implement tax policies and regulations that provide sufficiently motivating incentives for corporate leaders to do what is right not just for their shareholders but for all stakeholders, including workers, communities, local governments, indeed, our entire American society.

Looking to the future, we hear a lot about solar and wind energy, electric vehicles, artificial intelligence, etc. It should not be lost on anyone that some other countries have acted more quickly in some of these areas than us to invest the resources to develop technologies and first-to-market product capabilities. China, in particular, has a track record of many past successes in low-cost manufacturing and process innovations, which should alert us to just how aggressively competitive they will continue to be. The bipartisan CHIPS and Science Act of 2022 is a step in the right direction, aimed at increasing investment in domestic high-tech research and bringing semiconductor manufacturing back to the United States. We must do more.

American government, corporations, and universities need to collaborate to develop a robust and sustainable national economic strategy that puts investing in America's technological leadership at the forefront of our efforts not only to reduce our dependence upon foreign manufacturing and vulnerability to supply chain disruptions, but also to achieve and maintain leadership positions in critical areas of industry, commerce, and security, to educate and transform American employees into the workforce of tomorrow and to keep America competitive in world markets.

MANAGING AUTOMATION AND ARTIFICIAL INTELLIGENCE

In acknowledging the dignity of workers, we need to act wisely in managing job automation, the use of self-service, and the deployment of artificial intelligence. No doubt, each of these business practices can reduce costs and increase capabilities but they come with consequences - not all of which are good.

Having robots install rivets onto pieces of sheet metal that will eventually become the housing for a home appliance will lower the manufacturing cost of the appliance and make it cheaper for consumers to purchase. But the workers who previously installed those rivets will be out of work unless they are adequately trained to qualify for, and have access to, other jobs. Self-service checkout at retail establishments reduces the need for cashiers and clerks, but it also eliminates many entry level job opportunities that lots of young adults depend upon as their entre to the world of work. Moreover, it denies consumers and clerks alike the opportunity to engage in polite social conversation which can nurture community connections. Artificial intelligence holds much promise to accelerate our ability to conduct complex calculations exponentially faster and with fewer errors than humans, to turbo charge scientific inquiry, to substitute robots for humans in high-risk activities, to create innovative products like driverless vehicles, and to be applied to other endeavors that we have yet to imagine in education, healthcare, law enforcement, and national security.

37

But AI also holds the potential to make some humans less inclined to learn and think for themselves, to diminish the role of ethics and empathy in decision making, to displace millions of workers, to hollow out workforces, and to eliminate the wages which support many American families and communities. Moreover, in the realm of politics, AI can be maliciously utilized to scale the creation and turbo charge the dissemination of disinformation and fake imagery, which distorts reality, misinforms the public, erodes trust in democratic institutions, and leads to political divisiveness and social unrest.

There are no cookie-cutter approaches to managing automation, self-service, and artificial intelligence. What is needed is collective input from government, industry, and academia to analyze the opportunities and challenges that jobs automation, self-service, and AI represent and to develop common sense, sustainable policies and protocols that enable us as a national community to exploit advantages and minimize disadvantages. Preliminary steps have already been taken with recent meetings between the federal government and tech industry leaders regarding AI. This type of dialogue needs to be formalized and empowered to act as incisively and quickly as the rapid pace of technological change.

We may also have to revisit the historic trade-off we made in favor of more and cheaper foreign made consumer goods in a throw away culture, in favor of a different calculus that employs more Americans domestically manufacturing, for a living wage, better quality goods that command a modestly higher price in the market but which also last longer, don't need to be replaced as often and can be rung up at the checkout counter by humans who can interact with consumers, answering questions, making suggestions and engaging in the social pleasantries that foster healthy human interaction. This would sustain more American workers, preserve the human dimension of purchase transactions, lessen our dependence upon foreign suppliers, and reduce the amount of waste going into our landfills.

At a minimum, we need to have a national conversation about how we balance human needs with financial and technological means. Since work is an essential part of what gives meaning to human life on earth, we need to ensure that technology and business practices enhance, rather than diminish, humans' engagement with work. After all, our economy is supposed to serve us as people, not the other way around.

STRENGTHENING PENSIONS AND SOCIAL SECURITY FUNDING

Until the 1980s, 'defined benefit' pensions were the most popular retirement plan offered by employers, funded largely by the employer organization. Today, only 15% of private sector workers have a defined benefit pension. They have largely been replaced by 'defined contribution' plans, which are primarily funded by employees who must choose the investments and absorb all investment risk.

Some employers may make matching contributions, up to a certain amount, but the amount of money available when an employee retires depends upon how much they contributed to their plan and the performance of the investments they chose. Unlike traditional defined benefit pensions, which enabled employees to estimate how much money they would receive each month because the payouts were determined by a set formula - typically based upon years of service, average earnings, and age at retirement - the more recent defined contribution plans make it difficult to estimate how much money a retiree will receive because of the vagaries of market performance and the lack of investment expertise of most workers.

The Pension Protection Act of 2006 required stricter funding requirements to help ensure that employees get paid the benefits that they are owed because companies have not always fully funded their pension plans. When that has happened, most dramatically with some steel companies and airlines, the government has often been forced to bail out the plans, shifting the company's financial obligation to taxpayers.

Although many public sector organizations still offer their employees defined benefit plans, private sector companies switched from offering employer provided pensions to employer-sponsored but employee-funded retirement plans, such as 401(k) accounts, because it reduces companies' costs and are less complex to manage than traditional pension plans. The change has shifted the burden of saving, investing, and market risk to employees. No doubt, estimating retirement benefits and associated funding requirements is complex. But you might ask, who is better equipped to evaluate the risks and potential returns of particular investments, to actively manage a portfolio of financial assets, to absorb potential market losses, and to estimate future retirement income - the finance department of a corporation and its financial management firm, or the average American worker?

Notwithstanding the obvious answer to that question, corporations, in their pursuit of profits for their shareholders, have succeeded in shifting the cost of pensions, the responsibility for managing financial assets, and the risk of market losses from themselves to their employees. So now, most American workers are on their own to plan for the income they will need in their retirement years. For those workers whose companies offer a defined contribution plan, such as a 401(k), they are usually advised to contribute the maximum amount annually. For employees of companies that don't offer any plan, they can open their own Individual Retirement Account (IRA), with similar advice to contribute as much each year as the tax laws allow, about which most Americans will necessarily seek advice from whomever prepares their tax returns.

You will recall that the worst economic downturn since WWII, from December 2007 to June 2009, saw hundreds of banks fail, millions of homes foreclosed upon, and Americans' net worth reduced by over $14 trillion. Unemployment increased from 5% in 2007 to 10% in 2009. The period 2007-2008 saw a one-third drop in the S&P Index, which had a devastating impact on retirement accounts. Most mid-career workers still had enough of their earning years ahead of them to make up for the losses in their 401(k)s and IRAs, but late-career workers planning to retire soon saw their retirement nest eggs significantly reduced with little or no time to make up for the losses, thereby relegating them to living on even less retirement income than they had estimated.

The problem with shifting responsibility for saving and investing from corporations, with access to the most astute financial experts, to individual workers, with little financial savvy, is exacerbated by the fact that approximately 60% of Americans live paycheck to paycheck, which makes saving for their future retirement extremely difficult if not impossible when trying to make ends meet for present-day needs. So under-served are Americans that right now, about 40% of older Americans rely exclusively on Social Security income in retirement. This dependence will likely increase as younger workers without defined benefit pensions reach retirement age.

With the aforementioned shift from traditional defined benefit plans, which guarantee a certain benefit amount upon retirement, toward defined contribution plans, which pays a hoped for anticipated amount based upon how much a worker has contributed and the rate of return they earn in the financial markets, Social Security is poised to become most American workers' only source of guaranteed income that is not subject to investment risk or financial market fluctuations. The importance of Social Security for Americans' financial wellbeing and dignity in old age cannot be underestimated.

Social Security was created in 1935 as a contributory insurance plan with phased in benefits for retirees. The program was extended in 1939 to cover survivors of beneficiaries; in 1950 to cover farm workers, domestic workers, and the self-employed; and in 1959 to cover disabled workers. It is funded by a payroll tax - Federal Insurance Contributions Act (FICA) - paid 50/50 by employees and employers, 6.2% each on wages up to an annual income of $160,200 for 2023, which increased to $168,600 in 2024. The self-employed pay a combined 12.4% but can deduct half of that from their taxable income.

Demographic changes are presenting a challenge to Social Security. Americans are living longer and having fewer children which is leading to an aging population in which there will be fewer workers to support each retiree in the future. In 2020, 17% of the population was 65 or older. That is expected to increase to 24% by 2060. During the same period, our working age population is expected to shrink from 62% in 2020 to 57% in 2060. The ratio of workers paying into the system per system beneficiary is projected to decline from 2.8 in 2021 to 2.3 by 2035.

The 2023 report from the Social Security and Medicare Boards of Trustees predicts that the Social Security Trust Fund, which pays retirement and survivor benefits, will deplete its reserves by 2033 and that tax receipts will only cover 77% of benefits. Moreover, their report also predicts that the Hospital Insurance Trust Fund, which finances Medicare Part A, will be depleted by 2031 and that payroll taxes will cover only 89% of benefits.

To address this financial challenge, the U.S. Congress can do one of three things, or a combination thereof: (1) reduce the benefits, which would create hardships for many Americans in the most vulnerable period of their lives; (2) increase the retirement age, which does have precedent and is not unreasonable since people are able to work longer in a now mostly service-based economy than they were able to in generations past in an industrial based economy; and (3) raise the payroll taxes collected, either through increasing the percentage from the current 6.2% employee / 6.2% employer contribution rate, which most Americans would find objectionable, or through increasing the annual income contribution cap from $168,600 in 2024 to a substantially higher amount, which would seem more reasonable since people earning very high levels of income can more easily afford to pay more payroll taxes. This last option might necessitate adjusting the benefit formula to cap benefits for the highest earning contributors who would be more likely to have significant retirement savings of their own and, therefore, be less dependent upon Social Security benefits.

In short, to more fully embrace the dignity of workers when they transition into retirement, we would do well to strengthen private pensions and better fund social security benefits. And we need to do this sooner rather than later because current trends are unsustainable.

HONORING MONTHLY, THE CONTRIBUTION OF AMERICAN WORKERS

Since it became a federal holiday in 1894, and thanks to the efforts of organized labor unions, on the first Monday of every September, we celebrate Labor Day to honor the work and contributions of workers to the development and achievements of the United States. The combination of a population with a strong work ethic, enhanced with the influx of hard-working immigrants, led by the ingenuity of business leaders and sustained through the continuous innovation of forward thinking employees, enabled the United States to grow at phenomenal speed into an economically powerful nation able to most efficiently produce goods and offer living standards that became the envy of the world.

The daily disciplined effort of millions of workers to competently execute their job responsibilities sustains us in the thousands of communities that together form this great nation and enables us to serve Americans generation after generation. That effort is so foundational to our existence that the people who expend that effort deserve more than just one generic Labor Day each year to honor their efforts. We would more appropriately honor those who work with recognition each month for multiple discrete categories of workers to honor the variety of contributions that they each make to sustain our shared national community.

Public holidays are established by federal, state, and local governments. Federal law does not require any private business to close or to offer paid time off, although some state governments may. Private employers determine which holidays to observe. Several federal holidays are widely observed by private businesses with paid time off, including New Year's Day, Memorial Day, Independence Day, Labor Day, Thanksgiving, and Christmas. Christmas is the only religious holiday that is a federal holiday, though many businesses allow employees of other religions to take paid time off for their religious observances.

Our current federal holidays are:

- New Year's Day on January 1st
- Martin Luther King's Birthday on the 3rd Monday in January
- President's Day on the 3rd Monday in February
- Memorial Day on the last Monday in May
- Juneteenth Emancipation Day on June 19th
- Independence Day on July 4th
- Labor Day on the 1st Monday in September
- Columbus and Indigenous Peoples Day on the 2nd Monday in October
- Veterans' Day on November 11
- Thanksgiving Day on the 4th Thursday in November
- Christmas Day on December 25

To highlight the important expectation to work for all able-bodied residents and to recognize the dignity that accrues to those who do that work, we could expand our holiday celebrations by creating one holiday each month tailored to honor a particular category of workers. For example, at the end of this chapter is a proposed sequence and grouping of monthly holidays to serve as a frequent reminder of the value that we place on work and on those fellow Americans who perform it, keeping our communities running smoothly. These newly created monthly holidays would effectively double the number of holidays for Americans from eleven to twenty-three, providing well-earned respite for millions of overworked Americans and embedding in our culture a foundational expectation of, and respect for, work.

Whoa, so many more days off? Yes, and if you look at the statistics, well deserved. The Organization for Economic Cooperation and Development (OECD) is a forum where the governments of 37 democracies with market-based economies collaborate to develop policy standards to promote sustainable economic growth. According to their statistics, U.S. workers work an average of 1,791 hours per year, which turns out to be 442 more hours than German workers, 301 more hours than French workers, and 294 more hours than U.K. workers. Let's do the math: If we assume a workday to be 8 hours, that would mean U.S. workers work 55 more days per year than German workers, 37 more days than French workers, and 36 more days than U.K. workers. Their capitalist economies are highly productive, and their citizens enjoy a high standard of living, yet they are able to achieve this without demanding so many work hours. So, yes, giving Americans 12 more holidays - the equivalent of 96 hours off - seems perfectly reasonable to treat our workers more in line with that of our European peers.

Here's another way to look at it. The U.S. is the only industrialized country with no legally mandated annual leave. On a voluntary basis, though, we average 13 days per year. In most industrialized countries, workers get at least 20 paid vacation days on average. In France, they get 30. So, again, yes - short of passing legislation mandating a minimum of 20 paid vacation days annually, which is unlikely to happen - far faster and easier would be to give American workers an additional holiday each month to better align time off for American workers with our fellow workers in other industrialized democracies.

While it is true that public holidays come at a cost, including reduced productivity, especially for manufacturing businesses, and supply chain delays impacting the delivery of goods, it is also true that public holidays also present opportunities, such as increased sales when shoppers can head to their favorite stores instead of to work, and increased marketing opportunities for businesses to create holiday themed travel and leisure promotions and holiday product discounts to increase consumer spending. How individual businesses are impacted varies depending upon the nature of the business. Some argue that the loss of production and increase in wage cost for paid holidays outweigh the increase in spending. Others argue that anticipated monthly days off will reduce workers' stress and enable them to spend more time with family and friends, facilitating better work/life balance, which makes workers happier which leads to higher productivity on the job.

A recent study by Forbes assessed a variety of factors that contribute to work/life balance, including average working hours, amount of annual leave, maternity leave policy, proportion of hybrid working opportunities, etc. Their data indicates that almost all of the best countries for work/life balance are in Europe. The United States didn't even make it into the top ten. So, to the extent that in one fell legislative swoop and stroke of a president's pen, we could bring the treatment of American workers closer to that enjoyed by our

European friends by way of 12 additional monthly holidays, why wouldn't we?

Considering that these new holidays would be designed around honoring workers, it would send an unambiguous monthly message reminding each generation of the important expectation that our society places upon work and of how much we value those who do work. American culture would be better for it. The following sequencing is just a suggestion.

CATEGORIES OF WORKERS	MONTHLY HOLIDAYS Dates to be determined	WORKER EXAMPLES
Emergency Services And Law Enforcement	**January** Plus New Year's Day, January 1st M L King Day 3rd Monday	Fire Fighters, EMS Technicians, Police Officers, Dispatchers, District Attorneys, Public Defenders, Judges, Law Clerks, Court Staff, Correctional Officers, Probation Officers
Governance and Public Service	**February** Plus Presidents Day 3rd Monday	FEDERAL: CIA Analysts, CDC Scientists, DOT Regulatory Staff, FAA Investigators STATE: Comptrollers, Health Commissioners, Auditors, Environmental Engineers, Civil Service Staff LOCAL: Town Clerks, Sanitation Workers, Parks Staff, Election Observers
Healthcare	**March** Aligned with Doctors Day March 30th	Medical Researchers, Doctors, Nurses, Dentists, Hygienists, Technicians, Optometrists, Pharmacists, Respiratory Therapists, Medical Records Keepers, Hospital Custodial Staff, Assisted Living Staff

Personal and Pet Services	**April** Aligned with World Veterinary Day last Saturday	Hair Dressers, Manicurists, Massage Therapists, Health Club Trainers, Homecare Attendants, House Cleaners, Landscapers, Snow Clearers, Contractors, Veterinarians, Animal Shelter Staff, Adoption Volunteers
Families and Friends	**May** Plus Memorial Day last Monday	Spouses, Partners, Singletons, Parents, Foster Parents, Grandparents, Children, Grandchildren, Cousins, Aunts, Uncles, Nieces, Nephews, Friends, Neighbors
Agriculture and Food Services	**June** Plus Emancipation Day Juneteenth June 19th	Farmers, Farm Workers, Equipment Suppliers, Food Inspectors, Lab Technicians, Food Label Makers, Transporters, Chefs, Short Order Cooks, Kitchen Staff, Servers, Bartenders, Baristas
Energy and Telecom	**July** Plus Independence Day July 4th	Energy producers, Power Distributors, Environmental Scientists, Network Managers, Cable Layers, Shippers, Line Workers, Web Developers, Software Writers, Cyber Security Analysts
Retailers	**August**	Product Designers, Merchandise Buyers, Import Managers, Warehouse Workers, Customer Service Representatives, Delivery Services Personnel

Education	September Plus Labor Day 1st Monday	Teachers, Administrators, Aides, Tutors, Special Needs Educators, Coaches, Custodians, School Crossing Guards, Speech Pathologists, Translators, Maintenance Staff, Groundskeepers
Construction and Transport	October Plus Columbus Day + Indigenous Peoples Day 2nd Monday	Architects, Equipment Operators, Tradesmen and Tradeswomen, Laborers, Pilots, Flight Crews, Aircraft Servicing Staff, Conductors, Track Maintainers, Drivers, Auto Workers, Mechanics
Military and Civilian Service	November Plus Veterans Day Nov 11th Thanksgiving 4th Thursday	Veterans, Active Duty Military and Coast Guard, Reservists, Community Activists, Project Organizers, Senior Center Personnel, Homeless Shelter Staff, Food Bank Volunteers, Readers For The Blind
Mental Health and Spiritual Services	December Plus December 25th Christmas	Psychiatrists, Psychologists, Therapists, Substance Abuse Counselors, Social Workers, Benefits Case Managers, Priests, Pastors, Rabbis, Imams, Worship Service Videographers, Therapy Animal Healers

What We Can Do

It is incumbent upon all citizens to become informed about the critical issues facing our nation and our communities. With our rights come responsibilities, not the least of which is making informed choices at the ballot box. To help in this regard, below is a Candidate Evaluation Criteria checklist that you can use to evaluate one politician as compared to another politician campaigning for your vote to hold public office. Assess them yourself and decide which candidate is best prepared and most likely to take a transpartisan common sense approach to respecting the dignity of workers.

Candidate Evaluation Criteria

	Candidate _____'s Position on American Workers	Yes/No
1	Supports policies which discourage off-shoring of American jobs	
2	Supports policies which reduce dependence on foreign suppliers	
3	Encourages businesses to wisely manage automation and use of AI	
4	Encourages strengthening of pension benefits to sustain consumer purchasing power	
5	Advances substantially raising annual income cap for social security contributions	
6	Advances a monthly holiday schedule to honor various categories of workers	

The information, data and statistics mentioned came from a wide variety of open sources available over the internet. A debt of gratitude is expressed for the hard work of all those people at so many different private and public sector organizations who spend countless hours collecting and collating data, researching information, verifying facts, and producing reports for public consumption, which profoundly facilitates the creation of an informed citizenry upon which our democracy depends. Among those sources:

Bible

U.S. Department of Labor

Library of Congress

Wikipedia

Time Magazine

Economic Policy Institute

National Archives

Forbes

History Channel

Investopedia.com

OSHA.gov

Britannica.com

IBM.com

SSA.gov

FederalReserveHistory.org

BusinessInsider.com

Honoring Our Shared Stages of Life

Taking a Holistic Approach

We humans share in common something so existentially profound that it should inform our understanding of how we can best shape public policies to most healthfully live throughout our lives.

Scientists and psychologists have a variety of ways of looking at our various stages of life. For simplicity sake, let's consider the following six stages: Fetus - Infant - Child - Adolescent - Adult - Senior. During each stage, we experience varying degrees of independence. Imagine a classic bell-shaped curve with one's age spread along the bottom horizontal axis and one's degree of independence escalating upwards along the vertical axis.

As a FETUS, our starting position on the curve is at the lower left corner since we have no independence and are wholly dependent upon the health and activities of the mother in whose womb we are developing. This means that we need to ensure that pregnant women can access nutritious food, medical care, and healthy living arrangements that best support her and her growing fetus, who is completely dependent upon the mother's wellbeing.

As an INFANT, we remain only slightly less dependent since, for example, we can breathe on our own, but our needs actually expand. Not only does the mother need continued support to nourish and nurture her infant, but the infant also needs access to a wider array of nutritious food, expanded medical care, and a plethora of items that infants need, from diapers to nursery essentials, to strollers, to the attention and affection of other family members in the home.

As a CHILD, we move up the curve a bit as we begin to exercise a limited amount of independence, such as going to the potty alone, imaginatively playing with our toys, brushing our teeth, etc. But we remain dependent upon our parents to provide all of our daily essentials, emotional nurturing, mental stimulation, a calm home, etc. As the child grows, they are able to gradually exercise increasing amounts of independence by way of developing relationships with friends, exploring their neighborhood, engaging in organized group activities like sports and scouting, going to school, attending a house of worship, using social media, etc. A child remains very much dependent upon their parents, as well as upon the supervision of their friends' parents on play dates, upon their teachers who stimulate learning, upon the coaches and scout leaders who help them develop athletic and social skills, and upon religious leaders who instill moral values and help their parents shape the child's character.

ADOLESCENCE brings even greater independence and an ever expanding circle of contacts within the community, while gradually lessening dependence upon parents as primary caregivers, who necessarily gradually relinquish control in order to let the adolescent begin to exercise their own judgments on relatively minor matters. By the time they reach late adolescence and early adulthood, they are able to make more consequential decisions for themselves, from pursuing romantic interests, to making educational choices, to exploring career options etc., preferably in consultation with insightful and supportive family members.

Once they are able to financially provide for themselves as ADULTS, reaching the highest points on the bell-shaped curve, they begin a decades long journey of living with tremendous independence, taking on increasing responsibilities, expanding their knowledge and interests, enlarging their social circle, exploring the larger world and playing a more prominent role in other peoples' lives. It's worth noting, however, that adults still retain some dependence upon others, including trustworthy employers, accessible healthcare providers, competent professional services, effective community organizations, reliable public infrastructure, trained emergency responders, elected officials who craft public policies, et al.

Later in life, as a SENIOR, one begins the inexorable, gradual descent down the other side of the bell-shaped curve as our independence begins to give way to a creeping dependence upon others, such as a good ophthalmologist to help with declining vision, pharmaceutical manufacturers for drugs to help manage chronic health conditions, an employer who offers flexible work arrangements, social security benefits to help compensate for reduced job income, a social worker to help navigate a plethora of senior services, homecare to assist with the daily activities of living, an attorney to prepare end-of-life arrangements, even a funeral home director to prepare our bodies for burial.

In short, though the degree to which we are dependent upon others varies significantly throughout our lives, we are never lacking in some degree of dependence upon others. As such, we honor ourselves and our fellow citizens when we and our elected public officials acknowledge our mutual dependence and pursue public policies that address the challenges and needs inherent in each stage of our lives. And who recognize that sometimes those needs develop earlier, perhaps even suddenly, as when one may be born with limitations, become beset by chronic illness, or suffer an injury that prematurely increases one's dependence upon others. We are all subject to the stages of life and to unpredictable events of life, which a compassionate society sensibly anticipates and provides for in its policies, practices, and resource allocations.

Let's look at how the stages and events of life relate to a specific public policy. Take healthcare, for example. We all need access to quality healthcare throughout our lives - irrespective of our financial, social, educational, demographic, or geographic status. Our ability to access quality healthcare should not be determined by how much money we earn, whether or not our employer offers health insurance, whether we have a pre-existing condition, or any other discriminatory factor. Everyone needs healthcare, some more than others, but everyone. So, a sensible healthcare arrangement in our society would provide timely and affordable access to all citizens, would encourage informed self-care to prevent the development of avoidable health problems, and would require regular examination and testing protocols to identify potential health concerns before they become more serious, debilitating and expensive to treat.

The importance of healthcare accessibility was highlighted in a November 2022 article in the Society for Human Resource Management (SHRM) Executive Network, describing a 2019 study of data from 2013 to 2017, which found that Medicaid expansion was associated with over 19,000 fewer deaths among older, low-income adults. Conversely, over 15,000 preventable deaths occurred in states that did not expand Medicaid. Clearly, expanding affordable healthcare makes sense morally and financially.

Currently, in America, too many people have to navigate a complex patchwork of changing health insurance schemes, discriminatory financial and age criteria, distinctions by employer and employment status, and a multiplicity of often confusing types of healthcare plans, options, procedure-specific prior approvals, etc., which leave millions of people confused, many without affordable coverage, force some poor to choose between purchasing groceries or medications, or sink patients deeply into debt while they are already overwhelmed by debilitating health conditions. Surely, American ingenuity and empathy should enable us to organize healthcare coverage for all citizens more simply, affordably, and fairly.

And it's not just patients who are not currently as well served as they could be. Healthcare providers are struggling to hire enough properly trained healthcare professionals. As reported by SHRM, studies project that by 2034, we will have a shortage of over 130,000 doctors across all fields, from primary care to specialty care. Nursing shortages are already forcing some hospitals to hire contract travelling nurses who can earn a significant multiple well above what their local, full-time counterparts are paid. These trends are not sustainable if we expect healthcare providers to provide the high-quality care for which America has historically been admired.

Consider some of the clinical consequences. Data reported by ScienceDirect.com indicates that for every patient added to a nurse's workload, there is a 7% increase in risk-adjusted mortality after general surgery, not to mention increasing burnout among nurses, which often leads to their premature exit from the nursing profession, exacerbating the staffing challenge. The U.S. Bureau of Labor Statistics estimates that each year through 2030, there will be almost 195,000 vacancies for RNs. These types of critical labor shortages and associated clinical consequences should compel public policies that provide incentives and financial support for talented people to pursue careers within the healthcare professions, including scholarships, tuition assistance, student debt forgiveness, and tax breaks, especially for those who commit to work in understaffed specialties or in underserved geographic areas.

Sensible healthcare policy also would provide more robust funding for cutting-edge scientific and medical research and encourage accelerated innovation within the healthcare industry to develop pharmaceutical, surgical, and other therapeutic treatments that are medically efficacious and economically scalable.

Sick people make for a sick society. As helpful as the disease-based treatment model of medicine has been for treating those who develop disease, we could all benefit if we directed more attention and resources toward a disease prevention model of medicine where patients are empowered to play a more responsible and active role in managing their health to reduce, or at least delay until old age, the onset of chronic illnesses which place a heavier burden on a healthcare system.

Over 2,400 years ago, Hippocrates wrote, "*Let food be thy medicine.*" More recently, scientific research and clinical studies have led many healthcare professionals, including Dr. Caldwell Esselstyn of the Heart Disease Reversal Program at the Cleveland Clinic, Dr. Francis Collins of the National Institutes of Health, and many other preventive medicine experts, to state, "*your genes load the gun, your lifestyle pulls the trigger.*" In other words, we may have no control over our genetic predisposition to certain chronic ailments. But we do have control over what we put into our bodies and expose ourselves to in our environment, which can either delay, or accelerate, the manifestation of disease. Citizens need to be informed about the possible consequences of the lifestyle choices that they make, and how they may improve or diminish their health.* Public service advertisements to reinforce the messaging would be money well spent to try to minimize human suffering and the need for expensive medical treatment.

It's also worth noting that, since our eyes, ears and teeth are no less worthy parts of our bodies than our other organs, it seems to defy common sense to have to secure separate insurance plans for vision, hearing and dental care, or for many people to have no access to vision or dental coverage at all. This is not to suggest that plans necessarily need to reimburse for expensive, designer eyeglasses or cosmetic teeth whitening. But regular ophthalmology exams, and prescription eyeglasses or hearing aids when needed, as well as periodic dental cleanings, and treatment when needed, should be available to everyone, just like physical and mental health exams and treatment. If there was ever a situation which would seem to justify a holistic approach, it would seem to be to provide comprehensive healthcare coverage for the whole body, all parts included.

Another associated example of a public policy that should respect the stages of life is adequate and affordable nutrition accessible by everyone, from nursing mothers to nursing school students to nursing home residents - i.e., everyone everywhere. Too often, we see 'food deserts,' especially in poor neighborhoods, where the only conveniently available food items are the least healthy, highly processed products that actually contribute to the development of chronic illnesses such as diabetes, cardiovascular disease, and obesity. It's not just common sense but also clinically proven that eating healthy foods can have a profound influence on one's health, can improve quality of life and can minimize the need for expensive disease treatment.

Better to encourage people to eat healthy food and make it affordable than to leave people ignorant of its benefits or practically unable to avail themselves of it. If people stayed healthy through more life stages, this would enable them to have more productive, longer, tax-paying lives and would largely delay until old age the need to use expensive disease treatment, thereby reducing the financial burden on our healthcare system and freeing up resources for those who need it sooner due to injury or illness.

No one likes being sick or disabled. But when it happens to some, to constrain their ability to access healthcare they need is cruel. Life stages-based public policies in healthcare and nutrition have the potential to improve the quality of citizens' lives, empower citizens to take more responsibility for their well-being, reduce the early onset of chronic illness, reduce the severity of certain diseases, lengthen citizens' productive, tax revenue generating lives, reduce the length and cost of disease treatment within our healthcare system and lead to a healthier, more energetic and happier society.

All it takes is some strategic, holistic thinking, robust research, continuous innovation, targeted public education, and sensible government resource allocation, and we can craft more common sense healthcare and nutrition policies that truly honor our shared stages and vulnerabilities of life.

What We Can Do

It is incumbent upon all citizens to become informed about the critical issues facing our nation and our communities. With our rights come responsibilities, not the least of which is making informed choices at the ballot box. To help in this regard, below is a Candidate Evaluation Criteria checklist which you can use to evaluate one politician as compared to another politician campaigning for your vote to hold public office. Assess them yourself and decide which candidate is best prepared and most likely to take a **transpartisan** common sense approach to honoring our shared stages of life with common sense healthcare and nutrition policies.

Candidate Evaluation Criteria

	Candidate _____'s Position on Our Shared Stages of Life	Yes/No
1	Advocates universal citizen access to healthcare through all life stages	
2	Encourages nutrition education in schools and public service messages	
3	Incentivizes grocery stores to invest widely in communities to eliminate food deserts	
4	Provides incentives for talented people to choose careers in healthcare	
5	Advances legislation to fund scientific and preventive medicine research	
6	Encourages citizen responsibility for managing their health and wellbeing	

One resource in this regard is my earlier book, available through the website StopEatingTheAnimals.org, which describes how human health and animal welfare are inextricably linked. On the website are links to several medical and nutrition resources.

The information, data and statistics mentioned came from a wide variety of open sources available over the internet. A debt of gratitude is expressed for the hard work of all those people at so many different private and public sector organizations who spend countless hours collecting and collating data, researching information, verifying facts, and producing reports for public consumption, which profoundly facilitates the creation of an informed citizenry upon which our democracy depends. Among those sources:

Navigating the Twelve Stages of Life, Thomas Armstrong

Statista.com

USAFacts.org

StrengthenHealthcare.org

Society for Human Resource Management

ScienceDirect.com

U.S. Bureau of Labor Statistics

Balancing Crime and Punishment

Preserving a Nation of Laws and Second Chances

No society has limitless funds to expend on the common good. Citizens in a democracy can influence the prioritization that our government gives to the utilization of our tax dollars. We spend hundreds of billions of dollars every year on police, prosecutions, and punishment, yet we continue to see unacceptable levels of criminality in our society, and stubbornly high levels of recidivism, which makes it appropriate and sensible for us to reevaluate our approach to crime and punishment, particularly the severity of incarceration of those individuals who demonstrate by their unambiguous behavior a wanton disregard for law, civility and their fellow citizens.

Most crimes that we read about or experience in our communities - assault, rape, murder, robbery, shoplifting, car theft, arson, possessing illegal guns, drug possession, driving under the influence, etc. - are violations of state law. Each state legislature uses its authority to create laws that proscribe certain conduct within that state. Violators are prosecuted by a state or district attorney and state courts have jurisdiction to render decisions.

Federal crimes are tied to a federal interest or a national issue, such as murder on federal property, assault on an officer of a U.S. government agency, theft on a military installation, federal tax fraud, U.S. Postal Service mail fraud, Medicaid fraud, Small Business Administration loan fraud, interstate trafficking in contraband, possessing a machine gun that travelled across state lines, kidnapping across state lines, importing child pornography, terrorism, immigration, and customs violations, etc. U.S. Attorneys or Assistant U.S. Attorneys prosecute these crimes, which are adjudicated in a federal court.

Some crimes, such as bank robbery and kidnapping, violate both federal and state laws and can be prosecuted by both federal and state courts. Usually, one jurisdiction will defer to the other, although the U.S. Constitution's 'double jeopardy clause' that prohibits multiple prosecutions by the same sovereign does not apply to successive federal and state prosecutions because the federal and state governments are different sovereigns - i.e., law-making authorities. Moreover, a crime that occurs over multiple states can be prosecuted by each state since each is a different sovereign.

Approximately 90% of all criminal laws are legislated and signed into law at the state level. How effective those laws are in disincentivizing criminal behavior, while treating all accused individuals equitably, can vary considerably from state to state.

It is estimated that about 90% of criminal convictions result not from the conclusion of a trial, but from a plea bargain in which the defendant doesn't contest the charge(s), or plead guilty, in exchange for concessions from the prosecutor. Although plea agreements in some cases may not be considered by some as commensurate with the severity or consequences of a particular crime, plea bargaining does accelerate the judicial process and saves the government money from having to conduct lengthy trials with many witnesses.

The FBI recently retired its nearly century-old national crime data collection program, Uniform Crime Reporting (UCR) Program, and switched to a new system, National Incident Based Reporting System (NIBRS), which gathers more specific information on each incident. Unfortunately, several thousand of the nation's 18,000 law enforcement agencies did not successfully send crime data to the voluntary program. So, the following data is from the older UCR Program, which is less detailed but more comprehensive.

According to the FBI Uniform Crime Reports, 1,203,808 violent crimes were committed in the United States in 2019 - 366 violent crimes per 100,000 inhabitants, of which aggravated assaults accounted for 68%, robbery 22%, rape 8%, and murder 2%. Firearms were used in 74% of the murders, 36% of the robberies, and 28% of the aggravated assaults. In the same year, 6,925,677 property crimes were committed across the country - 2,109 property crimes per 100,000 inhabitants, resulting in property losses of $16 Billion. Law enforcement made 10,085,207 arrests, of which 495,871 were for violent crimes, and 1,074,367 were for property crimes. The highest number of arrests were for drug abuse violations, 1,558,862; driving under the influence, 1,024,508; and larceny theft, 813,073. Nearly 73% of those arrested were males, 69% of all persons arrested were White, 27% were Black or African American, and the remaining 4% were of other races.

Although this level of criminality in our society is hard to comprehend, those statistics are not the complete picture because, according to the Bureau of Justice Statistics, only 40.9% of violent crimes and 32.5% of household property crimes were actually reported to authorities in 2019. And of the crimes that were reported to police, the FBI clearance rate - the share of cases each year that are closed, or cleared, through the arrest, charging, and referral of a suspect for prosecution, or due to exceptional circumstances such as the death of a suspect, or a victim's refusal to cooperate with a prosecution - shows that police nationwide cleared 45.5% of violent crimes that were reported to them and 17.2% of the property crimes that came to their attention.

According to the FBI, the most frequently solved violent crime is homicide, with approximately six out of ten murders and non-negligent manslaughters cleared - which means that four out of ten murders and non-negligent homicides go unsolved. So, an untold number of murderers continue living freely in our communities.

The case clearance rate was lower for aggravated assault at 52%, for rape at 33% and for robbery at 30%. With regard to property crime, law enforcement agencies cleared 18% of larcenies/thefts, 14% of burglaries, and 14% of motor vehicle thefts. That means, for example, that 86% of vehicle thefts go unsolved, with yet even more thieves living freely in our communities. Nearly every day, we are reminded of retail theft that has compelled many stores to put consumer products under lock-and-key or to physically move out of certain neighborhoods. Thanks to the growing sophistication of organized criminal gangs and under-regulated online marketplaces where criminals can sell stolen merchandise, retailers lose billions of dollars, and consumers end up footing the bill in higher prices for stores to make up for merchandise theft.

Let's look at some comparative crime statistics. The researchers at Statista report that in 2020, there were 21,570 homicides in the United States, the vast majority of which were male and over half of whom were African American. The U.S. murder rate stood at 6.5 per 100,000 people, as compared to Canada at just 1.8, or England and Wales at an even lower 1.22 per 100,000 people. The European Union - where 118 million more people live, and live more densely, than in the United States - has far less violent crime and fewer gun deaths. According to the Institute for Health Metrics and Evaluation, the U.S. homicide rate is 6.2 times greater than in the EU.

Behind these statistics is real flesh-and-blood suffering and premature death of our fellow men, women, and children, our relatives, friends, coworkers, and neighbors, with consequent emotional devastation to their families and psychic injury to their communities. It reflects a horrible fact about America to which we have sadly grown accustomed to our own detriment. Whether we want to admit it or not, amidst the land of liberty and abundance co-exists a dimension of American life characterized by depravity, destruction, and death.

The injustice and inhumanity of it continue, though not for lack of trying to stop it. According to the Bureau of Justice Statistics, we spent $295.6 Billion on corrections and criminal justice in 2016, split among $142.5 Billion for police protection, $88.5 Billion on corrections, and $64.7 Billion on the judicial system. With 2.2 Million incarcerated individuals, that works out to taxpayers spending about $134,400 per prisoner or detainee. According to the Johns Hopkins Bloomberg School of Health, just on incarceration of adults convicted of sex crimes against children under 18, just that one category of crime, the government spent $5.4 Billion at the state and federal level. These are staggering sums of money spent yearly on problems that persist nonetheless to the ruination of far too many Americans' lives.

According to the National Institute of Corrections, the penal population in the U.S. of 2.2 Million adults is by far the largest in the world, with just under one-quarter of the world's prisoners held in American prisons. Nearly 1 out of every 100 adults in the U.S. is in prison or jail - 5 to 10 times higher than the rates in Western Europe and other democracies. What is going on in our beloved America? Our prison population is largely made up of males under the age of 40, disproportionately minority, poorly educated, and many with drug or alcohol addiction, mental illness, and/or lack of work preparation or experience.

What makes our U.S. expenditures on criminal justice and corrections all the more galling is the level of recidivism. According to the Bureau of Justice statistics, 70% of prisoners are rearrested within five years of their prison release. Recidivism rates are highest for those first arrested as teenagers and decline to less than 30% for those first arrested at 40 years of age or older. Think about the duplicative efforts this puts upon our law enforcement agencies, which have to devote personnel and resources to recapture and re-arrest the same criminals. Police officers can feel like they're repeatedly building castles in the sand. And think about the burden on our court system through which the criminals have to be repeatedly prosecuted and processed. The financial, social, and psychic impact of chasing the same bad actors again and again, putting them through a revolving door judicial system, and building more elaborate prisons to incarcerate them, while offering just a modicum of justice to their traumatized victims, is difficult to describe or to comprehend.

And in spite of all of these efforts and expenditures, year-in and year-out, Americans continue to suffer horrifying numbers of murders, rapes, robberies, violent assaults, and property crimes. Something is clearly wrong with this dimension of American life. We should be outraged. And outraged enough to demand that our government leaders deploy more effective strategies for reducing crime and implementing behavior changing punishment.

The idea of being locked up in prison and losing one's freedom is a powerful deterrent to crime for most Americans. But not for some. The 1960s adage, *"Don't do the crime, if you can't do the time,"* isn't persuasive with a certain segment of the population. Indeed, given the aforementioned high level of recidivism, it's apparent that imprisonment is much less of a sacrifice for them than it would be for most of us. Some, in fact, thrive in prison, creating their own little fiefdoms and even operating illicit outside businesses from inside the prison.

Thanks to our tax dollars, prisoners enjoy free medical care and dental care. They receive medications based upon need rather than ability to pay. They have access to a gym and plenty of time to exercise to stay fit. They can avail themselves of books to read and movies to watch thanks to the learning and entertainment resources purchased by prison libraries. With all of their free time in prison, they can even study to get their GED or college degree and, in some cases, a law degree.

Which working family in America wouldn't mind such free resources and free time to improve themselves? Which family wouldn't mind having breakfast, lunch and dinner served on the house, every day? Or to have their clothes and bedding laundered for nothing? For all of these resources, economic

68

benefits, and privileges that law-abiding citizens have to secure and pay for themselves, the criminals get handed to them for free. Are we fools?

The average cost to sustain each prisoner is equivalent to the compensation for a teacher, coach, medical technician, emergency responder, and a whole host of vital service providers whose positions we often feel budget constrained to eliminate in many of our communities. Laying off teachers who prepare our children to lead respectable lives in favor of sustaining criminals who act with a wanton disregard for our lives doesn't make sense. Closing firehouses while housing arsonists free of charge is not sensible public policy. Cutting the budgets of emergency responders while criminals continue to create emergencies defies logic. Unless we change our priorities, these ill-advised practices will continue to exact a stupefying toll on the quality of life of law-abiding Americans.

In our past noble attempts to avoid cruel and unusual punishment, we have erred in the hope that if we don't make criminals' detention too harsh, if we keep them well fed and healthy, if we provide them with entertainment and exercise and plenty of rest each night, if we give them an opportunity to learn, maybe even acquire some legitimate skills; then when they leave prison, they'll become the fine upstanding citizens that they otherwise would have been had it not been for their difficult childhoods, underserved neighborhoods, lousy schools, dearth of job opportunities and absence of positive role models.

Maybe, just maybe, it's time to admit that we were wrong, that we were hoping against hope, that we were trying to assuage our collective guilt for the deplorable state of some of our communities in which far too many children grow up, and adults struggle. With more than two-thirds of prisoners engaging in activities that lead to them being re-arrested after their release from prison, and half of them being convicted and going back to prison, it's pretty clear that a majority of criminals are incapable of becoming upstanding citizens. For all that we are spending on them as a society, we're getting a lousy return on our investment (ROI). And the longer we keep providing such generous imprisonment benefits for a population that will keep abusing our society, the more foolish is our throwing good money after bad.

We live in a time when federal programs for children, the mentally ill, the poor, and the elderly are periodically cut back, when state agencies often find themselves eliminating positions, localities reducing services, public colleges raising tuitions, and local governments sometimes balancing their budgets by laying off teachers, closing fire stations and downsizing police forces. We need to reassess our priorities and align them with what we should sensibly seek for our common good. That includes making some tough decisions about balancing crime and punishment because the current arrangements have not been working.

In undertaking such a task, we would not be encouraging our politicians to be needlessly harsh just for the sake of being harsh toward criminals. We would be encouraging them to use more common sense in allocating resources and crafting programs for society's common good. That can start with contrasting each politician's posture toward criminals' care with their attitude toward the plight of the working poor in our society. They work diligently, often in mind numbing or physically demanding jobs, to eke out a subsistence living for themselves and their families. Many of them cannot afford health insurance, dental services, health club memberships, family nights out at the movies, etc. Sometimes, they must skip meals or medications to make ends meet until the end of the month. They often don't have the energy, let alone the money, to work out at a gym to maintain their health. Internet connected computers are a luxury; even more so, the free time to take advantage of them when they're working two or three jobs just to meet basic living needs.

Our politicians need to appreciate that millions of law abiding people in our country survive paycheck to modest paycheck, living lives of financial insecurity, yet are not afforded anywhere near the level of benefits that government provides to the criminals who rape and pillage our communities. The vast majority of the poor don't resort to drugs, robbery, violence, or murder to gain an advantage over their fellow citizens, yet we give them so little, while at the same time, we give to the law breakers so much. Something is terribly wrong and patently unjust with this equation.

Some may argue that this suggested approach to realign public priorities and resources for the common good is 'simplistic.' I would argue that it is 'simple.' Society should reward universally acknowledged good behavior and punish universally recognized bad behavior. Currently, we are doing the opposite. We may not have intended to craft arrangements that are so counter intuitive, demoralizing, and unfair, but what has evolved over time, however well-intentioned it once may have been, has yielded negative unintended consequences that deserve to be corrected. Now is none too soon to make tough and urgently needed decisions about how we balance crime and punishment in our society.

While it is true that much crime correlates with miserable childhoods, a dearth of education and job opportunities, and an absence of hope of being able to emerge from lives of deprivation and depravity, not everyone from such challenging life circumstances resorts to criminal activities. Indeed, most do not and instead elect to carve out modest but legitimate paths to survival and advancement. So, the arguments offered by some that we need to make accommodations for criminals from underprivileged backgrounds ring hollow in the face of actual experience. In an admittedly imperfect world of growing needs and limited resources, I would submit that we may just have to accept that people, irrespective of the advantages or disadvantages of their particular life circumstances, make decisions and take actions for which they, as free moral agents, need to be held accountable. And that accountability to society needs to be swift and sure to effectively deter aberrant and criminal behavior.

Such a tough stance toward crime and punishment is not to imply that we shouldn't seek to improve the deficient circumstances of disadvantaged Americans, with special urgency for our young people, who find themselves in dysfunctional home environments, failing schools, and miserable communities. But it is to say that there is no *quid pro quo* - that until we improve the lot of some to a certain standard of living, we can't hold them accountable for their actions.

Being born into modest life circumstances, or being dealt a bad hand in life, does not confer exemptions from complying with our laws, anymore than an advantaged person should not be allowed exceptions for bad behavior. It is not cruel for our society to hold that, absent severe psychological infirmity, the law, our practical defenses under it, and individual accountability should apply equally to everyone. And for repeat offenders, it seems a matter of common sense that, after society has extended its helping hand once, those who bite it should be dealt with firmly and wisely in order to protect our law-abiding citizens, to better allocate our society's limited resources to those more deserving and to get a better ROI on our tax expenditures.

Considering the staggering costs that crime continues to impose on our citizens and our budgets, perhaps we can agree on some common sense ideas to change current practices. Some of these ideas have been considered, and others have been attempted on a limited scale. Here are a few offered for further discussion and consideration by our elected representatives.

FIRST, unburden our correctional system of drug-only offenders and put them into drug treatment facilities. Give these poor souls who, by dint of psychology or circumstances, are addicted to drugs, the healing treatment they need and provide them with the life skills to reintegrate into society as healthy, self-respecting citizens. This could include providing underprivileged African Americans reparations in the form of tuition assistance for vocational training to address the legacy of slavery that still retards the progress of many members of that minority community. Over time, these educational and rehabilitative programs, if used, could provide more attractive, legitimate, rather than criminal, paths to making a respectable life for oneself, presumably reducing prosecutions, incarcerations, and required prison capacity in our society. Immediate benefits would include local law enforcement being able to focus more on violent crime, terrorism, and property crime, and over burdened prosecutors being less compelled to resort to plea bargains to keep from falling under the weight of caseloads, thereby empowering them to bring to trial more serious criminal cases.

SECOND, while it's appropriate to distinguish classes of adult prisoner populations - such as those convicted of white-collar crimes, property crimes, and violent crimes – it's also necessary to separate first-time offenders from repeat offenders. The same rationale of housing prisoners in separate facilities equipped for each level of security that their criminal dispositions require would apply in separating first-time offenders - with a presumed greater likelihood of rehabilitation - from repeat offenders with a demonstrably entrenched criminal mind. It's counter productive to taint the first-time prisoner population with the mentality of hardened criminals serving multiple sentences. Moreover, it is merciful to give first-time offenders a chance to mend their ways, and it is no less just to refuse the pleas for mercy from those who repeatedly spurn it.

THIRD, incarcerate juvenile offenders in military-style boot camps instead of prisons or detention centers. It's not enough to simply separate our criminally convicted youth from adult prisoners whose influence could sink them more deeply into aberrant behavior. We must go further, as others have suggested and some have attempted, by assigning them to military-style boot camps where they can undergo a rigorous rehabilitative regime intended to instill self-esteem, self-respect, and self-discipline. If we catch them early, before their hearts have hardened, and work proactively to equip them with positive character shaping experiences, as well as life skills necessary to pull themselves up legitimately from situations of poverty, joblessness, and desperation, we can literally save lives – theirs and their otherwise potential future crime victims.

FOURTH, create powerful, compelling incentives against repeatedly committing crimes. Limit plea bargains, reduced sentences, and prison-capacity driven probations. Make repeat offenders' going to prison truly frightening – not by middle class family standards but by the standards of the street. Tough sentencing, no visitation rights, and prisons that function more like Geneva Convention compliant POW camps. Make prisoners work long six-day weeks, teach violent offenders conflict resolution skills, and let any prisoner eligible for eventual release learn a legitimate trade so that they can legally provide for themselves on the outside. Chronic repeat offenders would receive fewer opportunities and fewer benefits. This will send a message to those in our communities who may be inclined to robbery, rape, murder, or other crimes to think twice about what 'doing time' really entails by increasing the deterrent factor.

We could embed into sentencing guidelines the concept familiar to most Americans from our national pastime of baseball, 'three strikes and you're out,' which requires that the batter relinquish possession of the bat and return to the dug out. In the case of criminality, you relinquish your freedom and go back to prison for good. Some states have various iterations of 'three strikes,' but the policy should be rolled out nationwide. The revolving door must eventually stop revolving for those whose unambiguous repetitive criminal behavior demonstrates that they don't value living freely among law abiding citizens. It is arguably our duty as a civilized society to be both merciful and just. So, after exercising mercy with repeated warnings and time limited incarcerations, by the time someone commits a third crime, justice must prevail. Since the thrice repeat offenders have rejected society's mercy, they invite upon themselves society's justice. Enough is enough.

FIFTH, phase in these changes in our criminal justice system in conjunction with public service advertising (PSA) campaigns that put anyone criminally inclined on notice that if they commit the crime, they will do the time, and it promises to be the most miserable experience of their lives. No more excuses of, '*I didn't know. I didn't realize. No one told me.*' Let everyone be publicly put on notice. It's obvious from the consistently high rates of recidivism in American prisoner populations that the loss of freedom and the current prison culture are not sufficiently powerful incentives to change behavior among street-hardened criminals. They've adapted. So must our incarceration – in the direction of the POW camp model – and our public messaging in order to increase aversion to prison, reduce criminal activities, and lower costs to society.

SIXTH, develop a public work-study program as work-as-last-resort for citizens unable to find legitimate jobs on their own. The need to be productive is a powerful desire in most people. And the need to make one's own living is undeniably compelling in a capitalist economy. To diminish the urgency of the former, or deny the opportunity for the latter, is to create incentives to resort to criminal behavior. Respecting the dignity of work, and the skills to do so competently, must be integral parts of any effort to create a safer American society. Perhaps not for all, but certainly for many, what we invest in training and public work programs will be money we needn't spend on more police pursuits, prosecutions, and prisons.

SEVENTH, reform our criminal defense services. In state courts, citizens accused of crimes have access to counsel in one of three ways: public defenders paid by the state or county; law firms working on a volume/price contract with government; or private attorneys representing paying client defendants. Even though our right to counsel derives from our federal Constitution, the burden of funding citizen defense in our state courts has been put on our states and counties – a burden they are increasingly unable to carry. As the American Bar Association, National Association of Criminal Defense Lawyers, and National Legal Aid and Defender Association have reported, the consequences of inadequate funding include staggering caseloads on overworked public defenders, limited investigation of facts to defend the accused, and insufficient access to expert witnesses. Except for the wealthy and corporations who can easily afford one or several marquee name attorneys, expensive private investigations, and costly expert witnesses, most Americans cannot - and we should be concerned about the consequent disparities in legal representation. There are no easy fixes but the need for reform of our criminal defense services is compelling if we are to have confidence that each citizen, irrespective of socioeconomic circumstances, can truly get a fair trial in America.

In suggesting these seven tough but common sense ideas, we cannot ignore the history of our legal system having underserved certain segments of American society. We live with the vestiges of an ugly legacy that has contributed to a disproportionate number of poor, under-educated, and minority citizens sitting in jail under minor charges, or wasting away in prison under overly harsh sentences. Our colonial economy's dependence on slavery led to the ruination of many families, our naïve embrace of individualism to the detriment of community needs, our suspicion of immigrants, our well-intended but misguided construction of dehumanizing public housing complexes that quickly turned into ghettos, our abandonment of inner cities and under-funding of urban

76

schools, have all contributed to the sad state of affairs wherein America holds the unenviable position of imprisoning the most citizens while, ironically, sustaining a more violent society than our peers in Canada, Japan, and all of Western Europe.

America is better than this. We are capable of building a safer society in which all Americans can receive more protection in their communities, greater justice under the law, and more effective spending of tax monies on police, prosecutions, and punishment. In order to achieve that, we must challenge assumptions and make tough decisions.

What We Can Do

It is incumbent upon all citizens to become informed about the critical issues facing our nation and our communities. With our rights come responsibilities, not the least of which is making informed choices at the ballot box. To help in this regard, below is a Candidate Evaluation checklist which you can use to evaluate politicians campaigning for your vote to hold public office. Assess them yourself and decide which candidate is best prepared and most likely to take a transpartisan common sense approach to balancing crime and punishment.

Candidate Evaluation Criteria

	Candidate _____'s Position on Crime and Punishment	Yes/No
1	Seeks to unburden our correctional system of drug-only offenders and put them into drug treatment facilities	
2	Advocates separating first time offenders - with a presumed greater likelihood of rehabilitation - from repeat offenders with a demonstrably entrenched criminal mind	
3	Supports incarcerating juvenile offenders in military-style boot camps instead of detention centers	
4	Makes going to prison truly frightening – not by family standards but by street standards - and embedding "three strikes and you're out' into sentencing guidelines	
5	Advocates running PSAs that if someone commits the crime, they will do the time, and it will be the most miserable experience of their lives	
6	Supports public work-study programs as work-as-last-resort for those unable to find legitimate jobs on their own	
7	Encourages reform of our criminal defense services to have confidence that each citizen, irrespective of socioeconomic circumstances, can truly get a fair trial	

The information, data and statistics mentioned came from a wide variety of open sources available over the internet. A debt of gratitude is expressed for the hard work of all those people at so many different private and public sector organizations who spend countless hours collecting and collating data, researching information, verifying facts, and producing reports for public consumption, which profoundly facilitates the creation of an informed citizenry upon which our democracy depends. Among those sources:

FBI Uniform Crime Reports

U.S. Department of Justice

Bureau of Justice Statistics

UN Office on Drugs and Crime

Google

Wikipedia

PewResearch.org

AmericanActionForum.org

Economist.com

Statista.com

Global Peace Index

NationMaster.com

HealthData.org

Institute for Health Metrics and Evaluation

AmericanProgress.org

USAFacts.org

Managing Immigration and Border Security

Considering Historical Decisions and Contemporary Choices

America prides itself on being a country of immigrants, which legacy is largely responsible for the country's unprecedentedly rapid development. But that legacy played out in different ways for different groups, creating opportunities as well as harms along the way. Most recently, we are seeing foreigners seeking entrance into our country in numbers never anticipated when our immigration laws were written, which is compromising the effectiveness of our border security, causing unprecedented delays in the adjudication process for asylum seekers, overwhelming the communities to which immigrants are being sent, and causing political divisiveness that is tearing the social fabric of our society. Neither the immigrants nor our country are being well served by current practices. And we are not alone in dealing with this challenge. Europe is facing similar circumstances with similar deleterious effects.

According to the 2022 World Migration Report, the United States has been the primary destination of choice for international legal migrants since 1970, mostly from Mexico, India, China, the Philippines, and El Salvador. Germany came in second, with migrants coming mostly from Poland, Turkey, Russia, Kazakhstan, and Syria. Saudi Arabia placed third, with migrants hailing primarily from India, Indonesia, and Pakistan.

Countries need immigrants for a variety of reasons, not the least of which is to sustain economic growth, but they need them to enter legally after going through a vetting process. The waves of illegal migrants trying to gain entrance is not what we, nor any country, want. For the United States, our southern border is in crisis, and something needs to change and fast.

Before exploring possible paths to U.S. immigration reform, a brief history of our checkered immigration experience seems in order.

BRIEF HISTORICAL BACKGROUND

In 1786 was established the first Native American reservation and a policy of dealing with each tribe as an independent nation. In 1790 the federal government required two years of residency for naturalization. It wasn't until 1808 that Congress banned the importation of slaves. Just over a decade later, in 1819, immigration reporting was enacted by Congress. The 1830s saw some of the most ignominious actions by Congress, with the 1830 passage of the Removal Act, forcing Native Americans to settle in Indian Territory west of the Mississippi River, and, in 1838, forcing Cherokee Indians on a one-thousand mile march to the established Indian Territory, during which 4,000 Cherokees died, historically referred to as the "Trail of Tears."

The end of the Mexican-American War in 1848 saw the United States capture additional territory and the people living on that land. One year later, in 1849, the California Gold Rush saw the beginning of migrants from China coming to America. The Transcontinental railroad was built by thousands of workers of various ethnic origins, though of particular note were the 20,000 Chinese laborers who, between 1863 and 1869, built the treacherous western portion of the railroad.

The 1850s saw tremendous harm done to African Americans, with the Fugitive Slaves Act passed in 1850, which increased the number of federal officers to catch runaway slaves and denied them the right to a jury trial. Adding insult to injury, in 1857, the Supreme Court's infamous Dred Scott decision declared that the U. S. Constitution did not extend American citizenship to people of black African descent, denying them the rights and privileges the Constitution confers to American citizens.

81

At the time of Abraham Lincoln's becoming president in 1861, the Southern Confederacy of seven slave owning states ratified a new Constitution and elected Jefferson Davis as the first Confederate president, laying the seeds for the 1861 to 1865 Civil War, ultimately fought over the politically divisive issue of whether slavery would be permitted to expand into the western territories, thereby leading to more slave states.

The Southern Confederacy eventually expanded to 11 states, out of then 34 states, with control over one-third of the American population. Mid-War in 1863, President Lincoln issued the Emancipation Proclamation, mandating that all three million slaves living in the rebellious states were to be considered free. By the time the Civil War ended in 1865, over 700,000 soldiers were dead, making it the deadliest war in American history.

It wasn't until 1868 that African Americans were endowed with citizenship in the 14th Amendment to the U.S. Constitution. That same Amendment, however, included a clause preventing Native American men from receiving the right to vote. This was yet another blow against Native Americans coming on the heels of the 1864 forced three-hundred mile "Long Walk" of Navajo Indians from a Southwest Indian Territory to Fort Sumner in New Mexico. In that same year of 1864, Congress legalized the importation of contract laborers, which facilitated the immigration of Japanese laborers to Hawaii to work on sugar cane fields. It wasn't until 1870 that Congress passed the 15th Amendment to the U.S. Constitution, providing African American males with the right to vote.

One of the more positive developments in America's immigration legacy was the 1862 Homestead Act, which allowed for any adult or head of household, irrespective of gender, ethnicity, or country of origin, to claim up to 160 acres of free land, if they resided on that land for five years and made agricultural improvements. This formalized a nation-shaping western expansion that began in 1803 with the Louisiana Purchase and ended in 1890 when the U.S. Census Bureau declared that the new country's western frontier had been settled, at which point the country had grown to 44 states.

European immigration to America accelerated in 1845 when a potato famine in Ireland killed one million people and prompted the emigration of 500,000 people over the ensuing five years. In 1860, difficult economic conditions in Poland saw the start of emigration that, by 1914, saw two million Poles arrive in America. In 1880, crop failures and an unstable political climate in Italy was the catalyst for the emigration of Italians to the new country such that, by 1920, more than four million Italians had settled here, representing more than 10% of the foreign-born population. My own paternal grandparents were among them, having emigrated in 1900 from Fondi, Italy, to New York and later moving to Massachusetts.

The assassination in 1881 of Czar Alexander II, who was Emperor of Russia, King of Poland, and Grand Duke of Finland, led to civil unrest and economic instability throughout the region. Moreover, Russia's 'May Laws,' which limited Jewish citizens' ability to live and work in Russia, prompted more than three million Russians to come to America in the ensuing thirty years.

By 1882, the attitude in the U.S. toward Chinese immigrants swung in the opposite direction with the passage of the Chinese Exclusion Act, which suspended immigration of Chinese laborers, and of a broader Congressional ban on the admission of any contract laborers. In 1887, the Dawes Act dissolved many Indian reservations, and in 1889, unoccupied Native American lands in Oklahoma were made available to white settlers. In 1896, the U.S. Supreme Court ruled in Plessy v Ferguson that 'separate but equal' accommodations for African Americans and whites was constitutional, ushering in a long period of legal segregation. Two years later, in 1898, the four month Spanish-American War led to Cuba's independence and the U.S. acquisition of Puerto Rico and Guam. Shortly thereafter, in 1900, Congress formed a civil government in Puerto Rico and granted their inhabitants U.S. citizenship.

In 1907, a diplomatic agreement between the United States and Japan saw Japan stop issuing passports to laborers while the Americans agreed not to prohibit Japanese immigration. However, California's 1913 Alien Land Law ruled that Japanese were ineligible to own agricultural land. Around the same time, in order to ameliorate a labor shortage in the Southwest, the Dillingham Commission in 1911 facilitated the immigration of Mexican laborers into the U.S. and exempted them from 'head taxes.'

With America's entry into World War I in 1917, anti-German sentiment led to the renaming of towns, streets, and some family names to sound less Germanic. Even German-originated dogs, like our now popular beloved Dachshunds and hard working German Shepherds, fell out of favor in America. In 1922, the U.S. Supreme Court ruled that first-generation Japanese were not eligible for citizenship and couldn't be naturalized. The Immigration Act of 1924 established fixed quotas of national origin and eliminated Far East immigration, while in that same year, Native Americans were granted full citizenship.

World War II had a profound impact upon our immigration policies and practices. During the war, over 125,000 people of Japanese descent, of whom two-thirds were U.S. citizens, were forced into 75 relocation camps.

In 1941, Presidential Executive Order 8802 forbade discrimination in federal government and defense industry hiring and training. At the same time, the Fair Employment Practices Commission was created to investigate discrimination against black employees.

In 1942, Congress allowed agricultural workers from throughout Latin America to work in the United States. Also, in 1942, the Magnuson Act repealed the Chinese Exclusion Act of 1882, established quotas for Chinese immigrants, and made them eligible for U.S. citizenship. In the mid-1940s, the War Bride Act and the G.I. Fiancés Act legalized the immigration of foreign-born spouses, fiancés and children of American military personnel. Also during that time the Supreme Court invalidated California's Alien Land Laws, which had prohibited Japanese immigrants' ownership of agricultural land.

In 1948, the government allowed over 200,000 refugees fleeing persecution to enter into the United States. Shortly thereafter, in 1950, the federal Bureau of Indian Affairs transferred responsibility for services to the individual states, and in 1952, the Bureau began selling over one million acres of Native American land to investors and developers.

An important development in 1952 was the passage of the Immigration and Nationality Act, which allowed eligibility for naturalization regardless of race, reaffirmed a national quota system, limited immigration from the Eastern Hemisphere, established immigration preferences for skilled workers and relatives of U.S. citizens or permanent resident aliens and strengthened entry procedures. In the following year, 1953, Congress amended the 1948 refugee policy and allowed 200,000 additional refugees. In the landmark 1954 case 'Brown v. Topeka Board of Education, the Supreme Court ruled that 'separate but equal' educational facilities were unconstitutional.

The 1960s saw more significant developments in U.S. immigration practices. From 1959 to 1961, Fidel Castro's revolution prompted the emigration from Cuba of 300,000 people, to which the U.S. responded with the Cuban Refugee Program that relocated many of them across the country over the next twenty years. In 1964, the Civil Rights Act enshrined voting rights and prohibited discrimination in housing.

The Immigration Act of 1965 adopted a new quota system allowing for 20,000 immigrants per country, with a preference for immediate family members and skilled workers. 1965 also saw the end of the Bracero Program which had enabled the temporary employment of over four million Mexicans. For eight years starting in 1965, 'freedom flights' from Cuba facilitated the entry of over 250,000 Cubans into the United States.

During the 1980s, we saw the passage of the Refugee Act of 1980, which redefined criteria for admitting refugees, and passage of the bi-partisan Immigration Reform and Control Act of 1986, which provided amnesty for established residents, increased border enforcement, enhanced reporting requirements for employers and expanded guest worker visa programs. In 1988, the Civil Liberties Act provided $20,000 of compensation, as well as a presidential apology, to Japanese American survivors of the World War II internment camps.

In 1990, Congress revised the Immigration Act of 1965 by implementing the H-1B visa program for skilled temporary works, with some provisions for transition to permanent status, and the diversity visa lottery for aspiring immigrants unable to enter through the preference system.

After the attacks of September 11, 2001, the 2002 Enhanced Border Security and Visa Entry Reform Act expanded the budget, staffing, and powers of the immigration enforcement bureaucracy. In that same year, the Homeland Security Act created the Department of Homeland Security by consolidating twenty-two agencies and bureaus into a more coordinated department.

In 2003, the investigative and enforcement arms of the US Customs Service and the Immigration and Naturalization Service were combined to create Immigration and Customs Enforcement (ICE). ICE operates under the Department of Homeland Security to enforce federal border control, customs, trade, and immigration laws. The organization detains, deports, and sometimes convicts specific types of unauthorized immigrants.

Nearly a decade later, in 2012, the Deferred Action for Childhood Arrivals (DACA) executive order provided protection from deportation and work authorization for millions of unauthorized immigrants who had arrived as minor children and had lived in the U.S. since June 15, 2007. This was followed up by another executive order in 2014, Deferred Action for Parents of Americans and Lawful Permanent Residents (DAPA), which provided protections for unauthorized immigrants whose children were American citizens or lawful permanent residents.

The year 2017 saw the implementation of several executive orders referred to as the 'Muslim Travel Ban,' which prohibited travel and refugee resettlement from predominately Muslim countries. Two years later, in 2019, the Department of Homeland Security finalized a rule that expanded the list of received benefits and other factors to be considered in deciding whether an applicant for admission, or for adjustment in immigration status, would likely become a public charge - i.e., dependent primarily upon government for subsistence via income maintenance or long term care at government expense.

In March 2020, when the World Health Organization declared Covid-19 a pandemic, the U.S. Government invoked Title 42 of U.S. Code 265 dating back to 1944, which empowered health authorities to prohibit migrants from entering the country if their entry could spread a contagious disease. This enabled U.S. border patrol agents to swiftly expel migrants to their home country or most recent transit country, instead of allowing them to seek asylum in the United States, thereby avoiding holding them in crowded immigration facilities as the highly transmissible corona virus was spreading. Title 42 ended on May 11, 2023, when the public health emergency for Covid-19 ended. In reverting to the previous border enforcement provisions of Title 8 of the United States Code, migrants can seek asylum only if they are able to cite a credible fear of persecution or other threats in their home country. Many migrants have to remain in Mexico until their asylum claims are decided. Those unable to establish a legal claim face removal and other potential penalties, such as five and ten year bans on reentry for those deported and being prosecuted criminally if repeatedly attempting to enter the U.S. without authorization.

An annual limit of 700,000 visas for quota-restricted immigrants was established in the Immigration Act of 1990. The annual limit of visa numbers allotted to applications worldwide is divided among certain preference categories of family-sponsored immigrants, job-based immigrants, and diversity-based immigrants.

Visa availability for the preference categories is based on country-specific demand and per country ceilings and is calculated according to a statutory formula by the U.S. Department of State. Separate from this limit are immediate relatives of U.S. citizens (spouses, parents, and unmarried minor children), as well as people granted adjustment of status as refugees. The same immigration act also created an investor category of immigrants. Under the EB-5 provisions, 10,000 visas are available annually to immigrants who are willing to invest a minimal amount in a new commercial enterprise, which will create at least ten full-time jobs for people other than among the investor's immediate family.

The immigration laws crafted three decades ago worked imperfectly and unfairly at times, but generally reasonably well in facilitating a relatively orderly administration of legal migration. But those laws written back then could not have anticipated the subsequent deterioration of social, economic, and political conditions in some countries, particularly to our south, as well as the inflation of poor migrants' aspirations for better lifestyles portrayed on social media, which has led to growing waves of illegal migration.

In 2000, apprehensions of migrants crossing illegally at our southwest border hit a peak of 1.6 million, fluctuated up and down in the ensuing years, and hit another peak of 1.7 million in 2021. Encounters with migrants at our southwestern border rose further in FY 2022 to 2.4 million and in FY 2023 to 2.5 million. Also, according to the Brookings Institution, in FY 2023, an estimated 600,000 migrants entered undetected without encountering border agents. And even among those migrants who entered our country legally, a percentage remained after the expiration of their visa. Some estimate that there are approximately 10 million unauthorized immigrants within a U.S. population of just over 330 million, thereby accounting for about 3% of the population. Among them, it is estimated that approximately two-thirds of the adults have lived in the U.S. for at least a decade.

War, gang violence, food insecurity, poverty, lack of economic opportunities, and unrealistic lifestyle expectations stimulated by globally available social media - exacerbated by transnational criminal organizations which mislead, rob, and exploit many migrants - are driving unprecedented levels of migration to North America, as well as to Europe. Immigration policies and practices need to adapt to these new realities.

Whether fleeing Central or South America, the Caribbean, the Middle East, or Africa, the migrants' desperation is heart-breaking, so severe, in fact, that many undertake dangerous journeys which cost some of them their lives. Their aspirations for a better and more secure life for themselves and their families are understandable. Their plights tug at our emotions, stirring within us feelings of empathy, compassion, and a desire to mercifully try to relieve their suffering.

But our rational minds tell us that everyone living in failed and failing states around the world cannot just move to North America or Europe. Already, we have seen that the sheer volume of migrants is creating chaos at our border, straining government budgets, depleting communities' resources, generating citizen animosity, and creating political divisiveness. Indeed, in Europe, it is empowering right wing, anti-immigrant, nationalist political parties. In the United States, what everyone at all levels of government have acknowledged for many years is that our broken immigration system is unsustainable.

A major bi-partisan effort in 2013 introduced the Border Security, Economic Opportunity, and Immigration Modernization Act, known as the 'Gang of Eight' Bill, because of its sponsorship by leaders from both political parties. It proposed many reforms, including: (i) establishing a merit based system for admitting high and low skilled workers; (ii) creating a W temporary work visa program for less skilled immigrants; (iii) allowing many illegal immigrants to obtain Registered Provisional Immigration Status, which would eventually permit them to become naturalized citizens; and (iv) ended the diversity lottery program. The Congressional Budget Office estimated that the bill would decrease the federal deficit, increase legal immigration, and reduce illegal immigration. Although it passed in the Senate 68 to 32, it was never brought for a vote in the House and expired.

Early in 2024, Republicans and Democrats reached a bi-partisan agreement on legislation representing the most aggressive border security and migration overhaul in decades. Among its provisions, it would raise the standard to receive asylum status, send away those who don't qualify, expedite cases for those who do qualify, provide critical funding to combat smuggling and drug trafficking, and hire more border patrol agents. Unfortunately, this carefully negotiated bipartisan bill got knee capped by a presidential candidate who wanted to use the border crisis as a campaign issue.

LEGAL IMMIGRATION

From 1783 to 2019, more than eighty-six million people legally immigrated to the United States. The desire to immigrate to the United States, combined with numerical limits and per country caps on family-based and employment-based immigration, has created a backlog of migrants who have been approved for green cards but are not able to receive them.

Approximately one million foreign workers and family members have been awaiting employment-based green cards, while over three million have been waiting for their immigration visas, which is now taking many years, in some cases up to a decade. Illegal migrants are managing to gain entry to our country, melt into the population, reunite with family members, get jobs, often off the books, and proceed with their lives. Meanwhile, those complying with our legal immigration process wait, year after year after year, up to or over a decade. How is that fair? What message is that sending to aspiring immigrants - do it the legal way and wait for years, or pay a smuggler and get into the United States within months.

The legal infrastructure under which people have legally immigrated to the United States has changed over time, with conflicting visions, political philosophies, and piecemeal legislation leaving us with an archaic and incoherent immigration system poorly processing outdated policy objectives. Neither legal nor illegal immigrants are being well served; legal immigration applicants are being unfairly disadvantaged, and our country is the worse off for it.

The United States needs legal immigrants to sustain economic growth. Changing societal norms and past economic success have reshaped America's demographics. The data suggests that as parents become wealthier, they invest more in the 'quality' of life of their children, such as their education. Since such investment is costly, many parents choose to have fewer children so that they can invest more in each child's quality of life and future prospects. Following the 1946 to 1964 baby boom, birth rates in the United States plummeted through the early 1970s, then fluctuated a bit in subsequent decades. The Great Recession of 2008 to 2009 marked another notable decline and birth rates have continued to fall since. Data from 2020 indicate that 43 states recorded their lowest fertility in three decades.

Fertility is important for immigration policy because, historically fertility and GDP per capita are strongly related, over time and across countries. As birth rates decline, working-age populations shrink, leading to labor shortages, which slows economic growth in key industries and reduces a country's economic competitiveness. It also means there are fewer consumers, which reduces macro consumer purchasing power in an American economy two-thirds dependent upon consumer spending, while also restricting businesses' domestic market growth opportunities and increasing their dependence upon less reliable foreign markets for future profits. The combination of lower birth rates, leading to an aging population with expanding life expectancies, is leading to an economically unsustainable scenario of fewer workers paying income taxes and contributing to social security upon which longer living seniors will increasingly financially depend. We need legal immigrants to be integrated into our society in order to balance these trends to sustain our country economically.

It is in our own national self-interest to fix our broken immigration system with a regime that encourages legal immigration and discourages illegal immigration. Failures with the former exacerbate problems with the latter. Common sense and compassion are required to craft policies and practices which balance the government's primary responsibility to protect our citizens and communities, with its secondary responsibility to do good wherever it can - within the limits of public budgets, community resources, and voters' expressed wishes, and in furtherance of our strategic and humanitarian foreign policy objectives.

That the world has countries torn apart by war and political violence, countries with incompetent and corrupt governments, countries overwhelmed with criminal gangs and lawlessness, countries plagued with poverty and disease, countries experiencing droughts and malnutrition, and countries with limited healthcare, education, and other basic services is a sad and sobering reality which provides a practical context in which to consider what we, and other prosperous democratic countries, can do to help alleviate some of that suffering while meeting primary commitments to our own citizens.

It is not an easy task to balance these, at times, competing interests. Clarity can be found in rediscovering who we are and how we thrive as a country of laws. Since a government's first responsibility is the security of the country and protection of its citizens, immigration must be managed within a legal and economic framework that puts the country's needs first and foremost. Millions of Americans can trace their lineage to ancestors who emigrated from foreign countries and entered the United States legally. Once here, their respect for American society's norms, their hard work, their willingness to learn English, and their encouragement of their peers to assimilate into the larger culture accelerated their economic, educational, and social advancement, which led to a higher quality of life for them and their children, and to our country's unprecedentedly rapid development into a network of thriving communities connected by a common language and shared values. That is the model of successful immigration that can and should guide current efforts at immigration reform. Opportunities are given to immigrants with concomitant responsibilities expected of the immigrants - a mutually beneficial quid pro quo.

BORDER SECURITY

Any serious immigration reform must start with border security. The chaos at our southern border is scandalous. It's a failure of our government, an affront to the human dignity of the migrants, and an avoidable hardship to the residents of the overwhelmed communities receiving the migrants. Since the safety and security of our citizens is the government's primary responsibility, this means that the federal government must use taxpayer monies to fund and deploy whatever resources are needed to secure our borders - personnel, equipment, physical

93

infrastructure, bilateral and multilateral agreements with other countries, as well as substantial and sustained support to the border states and the communities nationwide receiving and providing services to the migrants.

This may sound simplistic, but just as we wouldn't tolerate someone illegally entering our home or breaking into our business, we shouldn't tolerate anyone illegally entering our states or breaking through our borders. Those who try should be accurately identified, respectfully turned away if they are unable to satisfy the eligibility requirements for genuine asylum, and redirected to a more simplified and navigable legal process to apply for entrance. This protocol needs to be implemented as soon as practicable, with adequate resources, including enough judges to consider asylum cases in a timely and respectful manner.

Moreover, the practices issuing from this protocol need to be communicated, in their native languages, to the aspiring migrants far more convincingly than the disinformation that they receive from human smugglers, who themselves need to be prosecuted and punished for profiting from the exploitation of desperate and vulnerable migrants. In short, U.S. Customs and Border Protection, as well as our border states, need to be provided with the tangible resources which they require to effectively secure our borders. They need to utilize these resources to develop practices that are respectful but effective, while compassionately providing short-term resources to meet the migrants' basic living needs while in our custody being processed or turned away.

Admittedly, having to turn away illegal immigrants, especially families with children, is heartbreakingly harsh, but it is unavoidably necessary in order to restore a lawful environment on our border and to dissuade other migrants from initiating their own perilous journeys. Only the human traffickers benefit from their disinformation and migrants' desperation. The exploitation and chaos need to stop, and migrants' attention and energies need to be more sensibly redirected to improving conditions within their own countries.

LEGITIMATE ASYLUM REQUESTS

United States asylum law is based upon international agreements prepared after WWII to protect people fleeing, or fearing, persecution. The 1951 Convention Relating to the Status of Refugees was drafted by the United Nations to address large migrations ensuing in the aftermath of WWII, but only applied to people who were refugees due to events occurring before 1951. The 1967 U.N. Protocol Relating to the Status of Refugees expanded the definition to include future refugees. The United States acceded to the 1967 Protocol in 1968 and subsequently passed the Refugee Act of 1980 to comply with our international obligations.

According to U.S. Citizenship and Immigration Services (USCIS), under United States law, a 'refugee' is someone who is located outside of the United States, is of special humanitarian concern to the United States, demonstrates that they were persecuted or fear persecution due to race, religion, nationality, political opinion or membership in a particular social group, is not firmly resettled in another country, and is admissible to the United States. An 'asylee' is someone who applies while in the U.S. or at a U.S. port of entry. Note that seeking a better-paying job or nicer living conditions are not among the eligibility criteria for refugees or asylees.

The law requires that every year, federal government Executive Branch officials review the global refugee situation, project possible participation of the United States in resettling refugees, and discuss the reasons for believing that a proposed admission of refugees is justified by humanitarian concerns or is in the national interest. Following consultations with Congress, a Presidential Determination establishes admissions levels and regional allocations of refugees for the upcoming fiscal year. Processing priorities are established to determine which of the world's refugees are of special humanitarian concern to the United States. If a refugee applicant fulfills a processing priority, the applicant is afforded an interview with a USCIS officer, but is not guaranteed acceptance.

As of this writing, the priorities currently in use: Priority 1 are cases referred by the United Nations High Commissioner for Refugees (UNHCR), a United States Embassy, or a designated non-governmental organization (NGO); Priority 2 are groups of special humanitarian concern identified by the U.S. refugee program; and Priority 3 are family reunification cases (spouses, unmarried children under 21 and parents of persons lawfully admitted to the United States as refugees or asylees or permanent residents (green card holders) or U.S. citizens who previously had refugee or asylum status).

EMPLOYMENT BASED IMMIGRATION

Approximately 140,000 immigrant visas are available annually for non-citizens, and their spouses and children. If they have the right combination of skills, education, and/or work experience, they may be able to live permanently in the United States. EB-1 visa preference is reserved for persons of extraordinary ability in the sciences, arts, education, business or athletics, outstanding professors or researchers, and multinational executives and managers. EB-2 visa preference is for persons of professions holding advanced degrees or persons with exceptional abilities in the arts, sciences, or business. EB-3 visa preference is for professionals and skilled workers. EB-4 visa preference is for special immigrants, including religious workers, employees of U.S. foreign service posts, retired employees of international organizations, non-citizen minors who are wards of courts in the U.S., and certain other classes of non-citizens. EB-5 visa preference is for business investors who invest $1.8 million (or $900,000 if made in a targeted employment area) in a new commercial enterprise that employs at least ten full-time U.S. workers unrelated to the investor. Immigrants who satisfy these criteria are welcome because their skills and experience add value to our economy and communities.

ASSIMILATION

Historically, the ultimate objective of allowing immigrants into our country has been for them, and certainly, their children, to assimilate into the larger American culture, rather than to maintain separate minority culture enclaves, which can perpetuate feelings of isolation among the migrants, enable the continuation of unhealthy or inhumane old country practices, hide domestic abuse, retard the educational and social advancement of their children and raise suspicions within, even alienate, the larger majority culture communities. It is understandable that newly arrived immigrants may feel most comfortable living in communities with fellow immigrants from their own country or region with whom they share similar language, food, culture, and life experiences. For the recently arrived, these enclaves can facilitate the sharing of helpful information, experiences, and encouragement as the immigrants make the huge and highly stressful transition to creating new lives for themselves from scratch in an unfamiliar environment.

But it has been equally reasonable to expect that the immigrants' children, particularly those born here, set their sights on assimilating into the larger culture to become more widely accepted as 'American.' It is certainly understandable that they may continue to speak to their parents and older relatives in their native language, but at school, sporting events, clubs, entertainment venues, places of employment, government offices, etc., they have been expected to speak English to increase their social acceptance and ability to navigate within the larger community. If the children of immigrants wished to enhance their American experience, they were well advised to limit the cultural practices of the old country to family events in favor of adopting the cultural practices of the majority American culture for their larger lives.

Life is made up of choices. No one forces migrants to come to America, Europe, or anywhere else. If they feel that circumstances are driving them out of their native country, then they should be prepared to adapt and adopt the mores of the country that welcomes them with opportunities for a safer and better life. As the children of immigrants graduate from school, begin making an independent living, and take on marriage and family responsibilities, they should be encouraged to leave the immigrant enclaves and move into more diverse, stable communities throughout the country where they can create their own American dream. Often, this happens naturally when circumstances within the immigrant enclave encourage their movement out, such as when young mothers don't want to walk up and down old tenement building stairwells carrying their babies when they could live a more convenient ground level life easily maneuvering from, say, a single family home to their driveway and automobile. From the community's perspective, within a generation or two, the immigrant enclaves could be reoccupied by a newer group of immigrants from another part of the world, or the value of the real estate upon which these enclaves sat may have encouraged the renovation or replacement of buildings to serve other community purposes.

There is no disputing that the history of immigration to America has shown that 'assimilation' - the process whereby the minority culture adopts the practices, beliefs, and values of the dominant culture - was the key to achieving the American dream by the first born generations of children who learned the language, socialized with others outside of their immigrant group, adopted American pastimes and developed lifestyles comparable to those of their American peers, thereby enabling them to benefit from full citizenship status.

But assimilation does come at a cost, namely, generationally diluting their original cultural identity. For those who perceive this as too high a cost, they may prefer 'acculturation' - whereby the minority culture adopts some majority culture practices while trying to influence the majority culture to accept some of their minority cultural practices. Unfortunately, acculturation is not as well regarded by most Americans as assimilation because acculturation creates the impression that the immigrants are not fully embracing the culture and traditions of the country that welcomed them and may be trying to change the majority culture along minority culture lines. Sharing traditions in food, music, literature, art, clothing styles, sports, holiday celebrations, etc., is a welcome part of our multicultural society. But attempting to impose native country laws that conflict with the laws of the adopted country, or continuing practices considered objectionable or inhumane in one's adopted country, are not welcome.

People argue about whether America is a 'melting pot' or a 'mixed salad.' The former was based upon the idea of unity built around beliefs and ideas, not upon race, blood, or sect. The nineteenth century essayist, Ralph Waldo Emerson, utilized the melting pot idea to describe a *"fusing process... that transforms the English, the German, the Irish emigrant into an American."* In 1908 was produced a play written by Israel Zangwill, "The Melting Pot," in which a character says, *"America is God's crucible, the great melting pot where all the races of Europe are melting and reforming."*

The American identity has been based upon the unifying ideals enshrined in the Declaration of Independence and the Constitution, which convey that individual human rights transcend group identity. In spite of ethnocentrism, racism, and xenophobia, which have been a sad part of our legacy, the idea of a melting pot in which immigrants could find greater freedom and opportunity made the United States the most inclusive and tolerant country in the world and the destination of choice for millions.

In the 1960s there emerged a competing view of America as a 'salad bowl.' Rather than assimilating, different ethnic groups were enabled to coexist in their separate identities, sharing in common with other Americans only civil laws and the marketplace, but otherwise keeping to themselves. The 'mixed salad' metaphor may apply to the newly arrived immigrants who may miss and long for some aspects of the country from which they came or who may have difficulty adapting to their adopted country and, therefore, choose to remain among their own. But the 'melting pot' metaphor needs to replace the 'mixed salad' metaphor for subsequent generations if they wish to be trusted by the larger communities in which they find themselves and to be able to fully participate in the admittedly imperfect but nonetheless dignity affirming experience of American life.

MUTUALITY OF ACCEPTANCE

The United States of America may have been a divinely-inspired idea bestowed upon Europeans, but the ideals advanced of what it means to be an American transcend country of origin, ethnicity, race, etc., and are bound up in the belief in, and the legal prioritization of, each individual and their rights. These ideals can and should be embraced by anyone who aspires to be authentically American and should supplant allegiance to any beliefs or practices which contradict this ideal. What that means in practice is that we long residing Americans of European ancestry need to challenge our ethnocentrism, and shed any prejudices it may have spawned, in favor of embracing the idea that America is bigger than ethnicity, big enough to include any person - regardless of the shade of their skin or the contours of their face, their choice of food or their definition of deity - anyone who adopts the ideals of individual liberty, individual initiative, and individual responsibility. These ideals have proven to be the basis of unity among many within our American culture.

Shedding ethnocentrism, and revealing the unconscious prejudices that often come with it, is not an easy task. We humans tend to resist change, especially if that change requires reevaluating what we once thought were established norms. Such profound change can only happen if it involves the 'head' as well as the 'heart.' As some have already learned, the best way to begin to question our assumptions about others is to get to know on an individual level some of those immigrants who appear so different on the outside, yet share so much of our common humanity on the inside. Instead of thinking of them by their ethnicity, race or religion, we can begin to think of them by their individual personhood, starting with their given name. Michael and Miguel, as well as Mary and Maria, may discover that they have much more in common with regard to their hopes, fears, and aspirations than they realize.

DEMOGRAPHIC IMPERATIVES

Demographic changes within the U.S. are hastening the need to embrace a broader understanding of the longer term need for immigration reform. According to the U.S. Census Bureau, whites are projected to remain the single largest group for the next forty years. However, in the coming decades, as our population ages and grows more slowly, largely due to declines in fertility, we will become a more racially and ethnically pluralistic society. This continues a long-standing trend. In 1900, about 12% of the population was of a race other than white. By 1990, nearly 20% was of a race other than white. That trend is expected to continue so that by 2060, 32% of the population is projected to be of a race other than white.

Moreover, our society is also graying. By about 2030, all baby boomers will be older than 65, which will expand the size of the older population so that one in five Americans will be of retirement age. By the mid-2030s, older adults are projected to outnumber children for the first time in U.S. history. At that time immigration is also projected to overtake our population's natural increase (excess of births over deaths) as the primary driver of U.S. population growth.

Without immigrants, as our country's natural birth rates decline and the working-age population shrinks, labor shortages would ensue, which would slow economic growth, rendering our economy less able to provide for our society's needs and eroding America's economic competitiveness. In short, we need to welcome and embrace legal immigrants and we need them to embrace our majority cultural ideals, values, and behaviors.

IMMIGRATION REFORM

In light of our country's history, needs, and values, our government's immigration reform should be driven by three equally important goals: Enhancing Our Economy; Executing Our Foreign Policy; and Extending Our Compassion.

Most people would agree that taking in a manageable number of people who credibly satisfy refugee status requirements is the compassionate thing to do. Doing so acknowledges our moral responsibility as a wealthy nation to alleviate the suffering of migrants facing the most urgent threats to their lives, particularly refugees of war, those unable to access urgently needed life-saving healthcare, and foreigners whose lives are at risk due to their having assisted U.S. diplomats or military personnel within their home country.

Building into our immigration posture practices that advance our foreign policy objectives regionally and strategically, and that build goodwill globally to enhance our leadership role on the world stage, is the wise thing to do. It strengthens our relationships with allies, enhances the effectiveness of multilateral organizations in addressing some of the root causes of illegal immigration, advances our strategic and economic policy objectives in competition with our adversaries, and supports our continued advancement of international human rights.

Inviting in people who bring skills and experience that can enhance our country's productivity and competitiveness is the common sense thing to do, particularly in areas where there are anticipated to be shortages of workers needed to sustain economic growth, which cannot otherwise be met by the hiring and training of our own citizens. This was the rationale for the H-1B non-immigrant visa provisions of Section 101 of the Immigration and Nationality Act, which allows U.S. employers to employ foreign workers in specialty occupations. Although the H-1B non-immigrant visa requires the application of specialized knowledge and a bachelor's degree or equivalent work experience, the concept could be expanded to apply to less specialized skills and knowledge, such as in certain sectors which often struggle to fill entry level jobs, including in home healthcare, housekeeping, agriculture, landscaping, delivery services, etc. After meeting certain requirements, not the least of which would be paying income taxes, making social security contributions, and not engaging in dangerous or criminal activity, over a reasonable predetermined period of time, these foreign workers, and their family members, could be afforded legal pathways to citizenship.

This was the idea embodied in the Deferred Action for Childhood Arrivals (DACA) program and the Deferred Action for Parents of U.S. Citizens and Lawful Permanent Residents (DAPA) program, although they were more limited in scope - not granting legal status but simply making applicants eligible for work permits and shielding them from deportation. If migrants who have legally entered the United States demonstrate over time by their behavior that they are responsible, law-abiding tax payers, we could naturally consider them to be prospective good citizens.

Conversely, those who fail to adapt to conventional standards of civility and community life, or engage in reckless, dangerous, or criminal behavior, would render themselves ineligible for consideration of citizenship. Naturally, we would need to provide immigrants with a thorough orientation to accepted American cultural practices and behavioral expectations and, where necessary, support to help them shed or replace unacceptable practices brought with them from their country of origin. In this regard, we should do a better job of providing a rigorous orientation program for newly arriving legal immigrants to educate them on conventionally accepted expectations of personal practices, from social interactions to personal hygiene, as well as community behavior, from group gatherings to safe driving. Not only would this facilitate immigrants' more rapid assimilation, but it would also reduce the frequency of unpleasant incidences with members of the larger community, which can contribute to prejudicial thinking.

ADDRESSING ROOT CAUSES OF ILLEGAL IMMIGRATION

Finally, immigration reform can't exclude consideration of the factors driving people to such desperate measures as to risk their lives and the lives of their children in making perilous journeys through jungles and deserts, or in the case of illegal immigrants attempting to enter Europe, across seas in which some migrants perish. The problems from which immigrants flee require a herculean international effort, cooperation and sustained levels of funding to try to resolve. Building border barriers may be an effective short term solution to stem the tide, but for the longer term, aspiring illegal migrants need to be encouraged and supported to remain within their own countries to utilize their ambition and energy to solve problems facing them and their fellow citizens there.

If we, and the other wealthy democracies, wish to stop the flow of illegal migration - which will get worse as climate change renders certain areas on the globe less habitable - then we need to do a better job of helping people advocate for and accomplish reform within their own countries to breakup violent gangs, root out government corruption, spread educational opportunities and establish sustainable economic activities.

A good start would be to shrink the demand for illicit drugs within our own wealthy democracies, which the drug traffickers in some of these poor countries are all too happy to supply, thereby enabling them to generate enough money to take over and terrorize communities, manipulate local law enforcement, corrupt some government officials and spread their malign behavior to other countries. The initiatives of multilateral organizations supported by wealthy countries would be instrumental to reform efforts and could form the basis for additional initiatives to tackle other drivers of illegal immigration.

What We Can Do

It is incumbent upon all citizens to become informed about the critical issues facing our nation and our communities. With our rights come responsibilities, not the least of which is making informed choices at the ballot box. To help in this regard, below is a Candidate Evaluation Criteria checklist which you can use to evaluate one politician as compared to another politician campaigning for your vote to hold public office. Assess them yourself and decide which candidate is best prepared and most likely to take a transpartisan common sense approach to immigration and border security.

Candidate Evaluation Criteria

	Candidate _____'s Position on Immigration and Border Security	Yes/No
1	Will prioritize securing our southern border with adequate personnel and equipment	
2	Will provide adequate resources for rapid adjudication of asylum requests	
3	Will base any immigration reform upon a three-tiered foundation of enhancing our economy, executing our foreign policy, and extending our compassion	
4	Will create American culture orientation programs and require immigrants' attendance as a condition of asylum	
5	Will provide pathways to citizenship for law-abiding immigrants already in the country and expedited deportation for convicted law-breaking immigrants	
6	Will create for nationwide distribution public service announcements encouraging mutual respect, civility, and shared common values to enhance community life.	

The information, data and statistics mentioned came from a wide variety of open sources available over the internet. A debt of gratitude is expressed for the hard work of all those people at so many different private and public sector organizations who spend countless hours collecting and collating data, researching information, verifying facts, and producing reports for public consumption, which profoundly facilitates the creation of an informed citizenry upon which our democracy depends. Among those sources:

Statista.com

USAFacts.org

U.S. News and World Report

Library of Congress

Census.gov

Wikipedia

WorldAtlas.com

BBC

Britannica.com

PewTrusts.org

CATO.org

ImmigrationEquality.org

WelcomeCorps.org

USVisaNet.com

BusinessPundit.com

NationsOnline.org

Brookings Institution

Preserving Public Safety and Gun Rights

Living Together Without Fear

The Second Amendment to the United States Constitution, adopted on December 15, 1791, reads as follows:

A well regulated Militia, being necessary to the security of a free State,

the right of the people to keep and bear Arms, shall not be infringed.

Courts have historically used two different interpretations of the Second Amendment, initially the 'collective rights' interpretation which holds that the right to bear arms is dependent upon militia membership. The idea was that citizens should be able to arm themselves to organize militias in order to deter tyrannical government, repel invasion, and suppress insurrection.

Later court decisions embraced the 'individual rights' interpretation, which holds that an individual may possess a firearm unconnected to service in a militia. A divided U.S. Supreme Court even ruled that an individual can use a firearm for 'traditionally' lawful purposes, such as participating in law enforcement and self-defense, even in the home. Objections to this interpretation were offered at the time, citing many longstanding prohibitions and restrictions on firearms possession consistent with the Second Amendment, but to no avail. Landmark decisions by the U.S. Supreme Court put into law the 'individual rights' interpretation. Given the influence of the National Rifle Association (NRA) and other gun groups, it seems unlikely that the more recent 'individual rights' interpretation will be changed in favor of the original 'collective rights' interpretation.

Nonetheless, in spite of the pro-gun lobby, it seemed a decade ago that the inexplicable horror of 20 children and six adults being slaughtered at Sandy Hook Elementary School in Newtown, CT, might galvanize a majority of Americans to take action demanding restrictions on who can own guns, where guns can be used, and what type of guns can be kept within the civilian population. Sadly, even though many Americans were outraged and energized, they were unable to thwart the powerful influence of the NRA and gun manufacturers on certain legislators.

Mass shootings are generally considered acts of public firearm violence in which a shooter kills at least four victims - excluding incidents of domestic violence, gang killings, or organization-sponsored terrorist acts. The United States has had more mass shootings than any other country on the planet. One-third of the world's mass shootings between 1966 and 2012 occurred in the United States. In just the eight years between 2015 and 2022, 19,000 people were killed or wounded in a mass shooting in the United States. The United States also sees the most school shootings in the world. The deadliest was the massacre in 2007 at Virginia Tech, which left 33 people dead and 23 injured. In 2022, we saw the horrific shooting at Robb Elementary School in Texas, which cost the lives of 19 students and two teachers. According to Statista.com, the United States had one mass shooting in 1982 and one in 2000. By 2022, we had 12 mass shootings. According to the U.S. Surgeon General, since 2020, gun-related injuries of all types have become the leading cause of death for children and adolescents, killing more kids than cancer, car accidents, and poisonings. Something is clearly amiss in our society, and it's getting worse.

The 1994 Public Safety and Recreational Firearms Use Protection Act, known as the Federal Assault Weapons Ban, prohibited the manufacture for civilian use of certain semi-automatic firearms, as well as large capacity ammunition magazines. The ban expired in 2004, and multiple attempts to renew the ban have failed. Despite the June 2022 modest

Bipartisan Safer Communities Act, and a Presidential Executive Order intended to expand background checks and encourage red-flag laws, comprehensive, nation-wide gun control legislation, including an assault weapons ban, has remained out of reach.

The Preamble of the Declaration of Independence, adopted on July 4, 1776, well before the adoption of the Second Amendment to the Constitution in 1791, conveys rights even greater than that to bear arms. The Preamble reads:

We hold these truths to be self-evident, that all men are created equal, that they are endowed by their Creator with certain unalienable Rights, that among these are Life, Liberty, and the pursuit of Happiness.

Are not Americans' lives, liberty, and pursuit of happiness infringed when they are threatened by guns in a classroom intended for their learning, in a theater intended for their entertainment, in a store intended for their shopping, in a house of worship intended for their inspiration, in a park intended for their recreation, or on a sidewalk intended for watching a parade? It is madness that Americans going about their daily lives are at risk of bodily injury or death from an onslaught of bullets.

Why won't the gun manufacturers and the gun lobby, as well as their campaign contributions-dependent politicians, accept that the fundamental right of life is frequently and fatally infringed by an absence of common sense regulation of guns and of those who possess them? Why don't they care that some of these weapons were intended for military use and often give the shooter more firepower than our police officers? It's an accepted convention that if you can't take down a wild animal with no more than three shots, you're not a hunter, so why would you need magazine clips containing dozens of bullets that can be fired in rapid succession? And since animals don't wear armor, why would hunters need armor piercing bullets?

Polling has found consistent majority backing for stricter gun laws since 2016, with 60% or more favoring tighter restrictions in every survey to ask the question since the 2018 mass shooting at Marjory Stoneman Douglas High School in Florida, which killed 14 students and three staff in just six minutes using an AR-15 style semi-automatic weapon and multiple magazines. The most recent polling indicates that 64% of Americans favor stricter gun control laws, yet here we are still without effective gun control laws as gun violence continues unabated in almost every corner of our society.

The right to life supersedes the right to bear arms. Conventional morality posits that we can like things, but we are supposed to love people. The current state of affairs has that calculus turned upside down. Some wrongheaded Americans love their guns more than they care about people. It is perverse and immoral.

As mass shootings and homicides tear through our communities, and suicides by gun devastate families, we need to align gun rights with commensurate responsibilities. The right to bear any arms should require the creation of a common sense national regulatory framework covering all types of guns. This would enable those who use weapons to enjoy their responsible use, while reducing the risks of their fellow citizens becoming victims of gun owners' irresponsible use.

American gun manufacturers produced 11 million guns in 2020, and American organizations imported another 6.8 million guns. The United States has less than 5% of the world's population, yet 46% of the world's civilian owned guns. It is estimated that there are more than 393 million guns within a U.S. population of 332 million residents. We rank number one in firearms per capita, not a statistic of which we should be proud.

In addition to having the highest rate of mass shootings, we also have the highest homicide-by-firearm rate among the world's most developed countries. These are symptoms of a society that is suffering. Although mass shootings receive the most media attention, they only account for a fraction of firearm deaths. In 2021, 48,830 people died from gun-related injuries in the U.S., according to the CDC. That's the equivalent of an entire small town's population losing their lives to guns. 26,328 were suicides, 20,958 were murders, 549 were accidental, 537 involved law enforcement, and 458 had undetermined circumstances.

Years ago, the Harvard Injury Control Research Center assessed the literature on guns and homicide and found substantial evidence that more guns means more murders. They wrote, *"Case-control studies, ecological time-series, and cross-sectional studies indicate that in homes, cities, states, and regions in the US, where there are more guns, both men and women are at higher risk for homicide, particularly firearm homicide."* They found that states with higher levels of household gun ownership had higher rates of firearm homicide and overall homicide. And for those who may doubt the data, they noted, *"This relationship held for both genders and all age groups, after accounting for rates of aggravated assault, robbery, unemployment, urbanization, alcohol consumption, and resource deprivation (e.g., poverty)."*

The grim gun facts have been around for years, and they are getting worse. We remain mired amidst an epidemic of gun violence. When fatalities of such magnitude are the result of a deadly circulating virus, defective consumer products, or failing infrastructure, our elected representatives are quick to pass comprehensive legislation and allocate resources to ameliorate the problem in the name of public safety. But not so with guns. The efforts are piecemeal at best, with so much political pushback as to retard progress.

It has been proposed by some gun advocates that we should put more weapons in our schools. That teachers or principals should be armed. Or off-duty police officers stationed at the front doors. The teachers' associations are opposed, and with good reason. We've already had mass shootings on school campuses with armed personnel onsite who were unable to stop the carnage. Schools should be safe sanctuaries where teachers are wholly focused on shaping young minds, not worrying whether they locked the desk drawer containing their gun, or whether a curious child might open the drawer and accidentally shoot themself or others.

Also, with regard to children, a recent study published in the scientific journal Injury Epidemiology looked at a decade's data in which children under 15 accidentally killed themselves or another child with a gun. Most of the shootings were in the victim's home, where in 80% of the cases, the gun belonged to an older relative, and the gun had been left unlocked and loaded. Adults acting this irresponsibly is outrageous. Whether guns are brought to school or kept within a home, our children are vulnerable and need adults to act responsibly, if not on their own initiative, then encouraged by regulatory requirements to do so.

The NRA's worn out recommendation to put armed personnel in every school in America is short sighted and impractical. It reflects the same convoluted thinking behind certain legislators in several states who passed laws allowing loaded guns in bars. There are even more states that allow weapons in restaurants which serve alcohol. People carrying loaded weapons while drinking booze in public establishments - this defies common sense. An alcohol fueled argument that used to end in a black eye or broken arm can now end with a trip to the morgue.

Within days of the shooting at the Sandy Hook Elementary School in Connecticut, two firefighters in New York State were shot to death while responding to a residential fire set by the shooter. Perhaps all of our firefighters need to be armed. Using this convoluted logic, every movie theater will have to have armed guards posted in the vestibule. Our shopping malls will have to be more heavily patrolled by gun wielding security staff. Using the NRA's rationale, virtually every locale will have to have people present with guns at the ready. Didn't we move beyond the pervasive presence of guns in the Wild West when we established police forces? Common sense tells any rational person that we don't need more guns; we need more regulations on the who, what, where, and how of guns in this country.

Regulations do not deny rights. There are all sorts of activities within American society that hold far less lethal potential than gun ownership, which require more knowledge testing, skills demonstration, medical evaluation, and government licensing, yet the sale and use of guns and ammunition continue to operate with far less practical oversight. The worst that an errant barber is likely to do is nick the occasional ear, yet the government demands to know more about them than we do of the people who purchase lethal weapons at gun shows. We require lawyers to qualify to practice law in each state, yet guns move freely from state to state with the potential for far more harm than legal documents or lawsuits. From driving cars on roads, to treating animals in veterinary clinics, to giving pedicures in salons, to dispensing prescriptions in pharmacies, we agreed as a society long ago that the common good is well served by regulating the people in possession of tools with the potential to inflict harm. Clearly, some of those who wield weapons in our society are causing grave harm to our citizens, to our national psyche, and to our global reputation. Americans deserve better.

Certainly, our society would benefit if our story tellers were more moderate in their depiction of violence in movies, television programs, simulation games, and online platforms, and if our healthcare system provided more resources for mental health screening and treatment. But the most important and impactful effort would be to better regulate gun ownership.

The naysayers posit that the problem isn't the guns; it's the mentally ill. The democracies in Europe have people with mental illness within their populations, yet they don't have nearly the level of gun violence that we do. The difference is that their societies aren't overflowing with guns like the United States, where we have more guns than people. So, make no mistake about it, it's the guns. The Europeans limit gun ownership with sensible regulations. Moreover, while they, like us, struggle to provide adequate resources for mental health screening and treatment, they entertain their populations with more bodily nudity and less bodily violence. One can only imagine the positive impact if our population was more exposed to love making than to killing.

But those cultural shifts take much time that we cannot afford as the slaughter of Americans continues unabated. More pressing and practical would be implementing an immediate protocol that will more effectively balance gun ownership with commensurate responsibilities in order to reduce firearm murders, suicides, accidental shootings, and shooters disposed to disordered thinking brandishing battlefield weapons.

Here are some common sense ideas for balancing gun rights with gun responsibilities, some of which have been attempted but which could be more robustly implemented nationwide.

AMNESTY PROGRAM - How about if every state government enacts a limited duration amnesty period every year during which legal and illegal residents can turn in unregistered guns and ammunition to law enforcement with no questions asked? Since many guns are illegal or were used in past crimes, getting them off the streets to prevent their use in the commission of further crimes should be a priority. Making it practical means allowing those who possess guns, including illegal immigrants, to turn them in voluntarily without fear of retribution.

BUY BACK PROGRAM - Every state could also initiate buy back programs to provide a financial incentive for residents to voluntarily turn in their firearms and ammunition with some level of compensation in return. This could be particularly targeted to families with children to reduce the risk of accidental shootings and would also reduce guns in homes experiencing domestic abuse or drug or alcohol abuse.

STATE REGISTRATION - Federal legislation could be passed to require all states to establish and maintain, to federally mandated criteria, state gun ownership registries through which any resident who wishes to own a firearm must be relicensed every few years, as many states do with driver licenses. This would cover all gun sales and ownership transfers, whether a retail purchase, online purchase, trade show purchase, import transaction, or private transaction, not unlike what we already do with the transfer of title of automobiles. Registrant information should include a criminal background check and a mental health evaluation, the results of which should be handled discretely for privacy reasons and limited to those with a 'need to know' in determining an applicant's fitness for gun ownership. While some may object to such assessments compromising one's right to complete privacy, in balancing competing citizen rights, our society has a more compelling interest in ensuring the safety of all of its citizenry by identifying individual citizens with a high risk criminal or psychological profile. Most folks would presumably pass with flying colors while identifying those few of legitimate concern. Of course, no one would be compelled to submit to such due diligence; just those who seek to possess lethal weapons within civilian society. Current background check requirements have so many gaping holes in many jurisdictions as to be ineffective. Just as we don't license pilots to fly our airliners across the country without ensuring that they are adequately trained and mentally and physically fit according to federally mandated standards, we shouldn't allow guns in the hands of residents unable to demonstrate that they are fully capable of handling them responsibly within their state and across state lines.

SAFETY TRAINING AND INSPECTION - With accidental shootings killing and injuring tens of thousands of Americans each year, it is not unreasonable to require that those who wish to possess guns undergo safety training and that the homes or businesses where they intend to keep their weapons be subject to periodic unscheduled inspections to ensure that weapons are being stored properly, lessening the chances of childhood curiosity, or worker rage, meeting up with unsecured weapons. The costs associated with safety training and onsite inspections should be borne by those requesting gun ownership. On an individual level, if you want to play golf, you have to pay greens fees. From a community perspective, if it's important enough to have our restaurants inspected for food safety, it should be even more important to carry out inspections for gun safety. After all, bullets do more harm than mouse droppings.

MANDATORY PUNISHMENT FOR ILLEGAL POSSESSION - Some guns and ammunition are so obviously ill-suited to hunting, sportsmanship, and self-defense that their presence within the civilian population should be severely restricted. Among them are assault weapons, once banned but which became legal again when a majority in Congress were unwilling to extend the assault weapons ban - in spite of law enforcement agencies across the country asking for reinstatement of the ban. Also to be banned are high capacity magazine clips and armor piercing bullets, neither of which are necessary for civilian purposes. And any guns not registered under the aforementioned registration program. We should have zero tolerance for violations of these safeguards for the good of society. Violations should result in swift and severe punishment to encourage compliance. The risks to life are just too high to do otherwise.

None of these arrangements would violate the Second Amendment's right to bear arms or prevent law abiding,

117

mentally healthy citizens from hunting animals, shooting at targets, or defending themselves. These arrangements would simply provide a prudent measure of regulation and oversight to ensure that the right to bear arms is being exercised by capable people using civilian society appropriate weapons in a responsible manner.

What We Can Do

It is incumbent upon all citizens to become informed about the critical issues facing our nation and our communities. With our rights come responsibilities, not the least of which is making informed choices at the ballot box. To help in this regard, below is a Candidate Evaluation Criteria checklist which you can use to evaluate one politician as compared to another politician campaigning for your vote to hold public office. Assess them yourself and decide which candidate is best prepared and most likely to take a **transpartisan** common sense approach to balancing gun rights and responsibilities.

Candidate Evaluation Criteria

	Candidate _____'s Position on Gun Rights and Responsibilities	Yes/No
1	Supports amnesty programs to voluntarily turn in guns without fear of retribution	
2	Would allocate resources for buy back programs to reduce guns in our communities	
3	Would support federal criteria mandated state gun registries and periodic gun relicensing	
4	Would require weapons training and safety inspections of all gun license applicants	
5	Supports a ban on assault weapons, large capacity magazines, and armor piercing bullets	
6	Advocates for severe, swift, and sure punishment for illegal weapons possession	

The information, data and statistics mentioned came from a wide variety of open sources available over the internet. A debt of gratitude is expressed for the hard work of all those people at so many different private and public sector organizations who spend countless hours collecting and collating data, researching information, verifying facts, and producing reports for public consumption, which profoundly facilitates the creation of an informed citizenry upon which our democracy depends. Among those sources:

EveryTownResearch.org

SandyHookPromise.org

BradyUnited.org

GunPolicy.org

GunViolenceArchive.org

Bureau of Alcohol, Tobacco, Firearms and Explosives

FBI Uniform Crime Reports

U.S. Department of Justice

National Institute of Justice

USAfacts.org

Statista.com

CDC

BBC

NPR

National Safety Council

Injury Epidemiology Journal

Harvard Injury Control Research Center

WorldPopulationReview.com

Office of the United States Surgeon General

Creating a Culture of Life

Applying a Consistent Principle

Virtually all societies have sanctioned *self-defense* and *just war* in taking other's lives - the former as a natural instinctive response to life-threatening behavior and the latter intended, though at times disingenuously, as a response of last resort to profound injustice. But some modern societies still grant, while others do not, government sanction to the taking of human life under the controversial circumstances of *capital punishment, euthanasia,* and *abortion.*

Many western European countries have eliminated capital punishment entirely, while in the United States, you may or may not be put to death if convicted of first degree murder, depending upon in which state you happen to live. In the medical realm, some believe that empathy for the intense suffering of others justifies euthanasia, while others consider assisted suicide a flawed response to such suffering. Around the world, abortions are allowed, or not, or only at different points in a fetus's development, depending upon the laws of each jurisdiction and considerations of the mother's health and fetal viability, which we have learned, changes as medical technology improves. At times, it all seems rather arbitrary since human life is human life wherever we may find it, including in a prison, hospital, or womb. This begs the question, *"Is there a consistent principle that cuts across life's circumstances that informs for or against these three forms of government-sanctioned taking of human life?"* I believe there is, though its implications may be unsettling to some current practices in civilized society, including our own.

Whether you believe human life is the product of intelligent design, a random act of nature, or a yet to be understood manifestation of the universe's energy, humans are incredibly complex, diverse, and in a supportive environment, capable of tremendous accomplishments. We are creatures whose biological processes share many characteristics with other life forms, yet we are uniquely different in our capacity to learn, reflect, imagine, and aspire. Across time and cultures, people have had a sense that we are more than our physicality, that there is an essence of every person that is contained within, but not constrained by the state of, our physical bodies. Humans' writings, ruminations, and intuitions reflect an ineffable sense that we are more than what we see, hear, smell, taste, and feel. We recognize, for example, that the veteran who lost an arm in war may have lost some of his physical capabilities, yet his personhood remains intact. Indeed, we often see those whose bodies have been irreparably damaged by accident or disease become even more thoughtful, generous, or inspiring human beings. They demonstrate to us that our humanness does not find its ultimate definition in our body but in what animates our body, what many consider our soul.

We can comprehend, even with our doubts, that there is a mysterious dimension to our existence that we can't fully grasp but before which we stand in awe. So much so that the deliberate taking of human life by another has always been deemed a significant act. Not that everyone's life has always been considered of equal value. Whether it was a primitive culture killing a member of its own tribe on a sacrificial altar, gladiators being put into a battle-to-the-death to entertain the community, a plantation owner managing through fear by hanging a runaway slave, a government subjecting prisoners to fatal medical experiments, or, even today in some countries, killing baby girls because of their presumed lower social utility than boys, humanity has at times been diabolical in rationalizing a lesser value of some people's lives. As human culture evolves, however, we slowly come to at least understand, if not consistently respect, the intrinsic value of every human being. But when it comes to murderers, the terminally ill, and unborn children, we seem to make exceptions to our respect for human life. Yet those exceptions

122

seem somewhat arbitrary – depending upon the intentionality of the murder, the painfulness of the illness, or the viability of the fetus. Let's look at each individually.

CAPITAL PUNISHMENT

One can certainly understand the desire to execute those who commit first-degree murder as documented by a fair trial. Who can't empathize with the gross injustice imposed upon the victim, and the inconsolable suffering inflicted upon the victim's family? There is truth in the sentiment often expressed in those circumstances that the murderer doesn't deserve to live. Yet in the face of such tragic loss, if we act on our desire for retribution, though we may rid society of one heinous criminal, we accustom ourselves to the pre-meditated taking of human life. To condition ourselves to accept as 'normal' the intentional termination of other human beings diminishes us as civilized people and undermines the value we say we place on human life in our society. We are right to condemn murderous behavior, to severely punish its perpetrators, and to protect society's potential future victims. But to take another's life, however sordid a life it may be, is to create the moral illusion that it's all right to take life under circumstances that suit us. This defeats the whole point of a civilized society that it is never right to kill – with or without government sanction - except in the aforementioned circumstances of self-defense or just war.

For our society's good, it is enough that we lock away the murderer in a miserable existence of lengthy confinement. For our humanity's good, it is even better if we can eventually find within ourselves the capacity to forgive. Not because the murderer deserves forgiveness, but because our act of forgiveness confirms the heights to which the human spirit can soar, even on behalf of our enemies. That excruciatingly difficult act makes us the more admirable people we are capable of being and serves to shame murderers who vainly attempt to deny the intrinsic value of every human life. Though

123

we are revolted by and despise the murderer's behavior, we should not diminish ourselves by doing with government sanction what the murderer did – end a person's life. For a civilized society, valuing all life is more important than extinguishing a particularly ignoble life.

EUTHANASIA AND ASSISTED SUICIDE

In the face of tragedy, we are often told that suffering is a part of life. It's a small comfort in the moment. But with the benefit of time to heal and distance to reflect, the truth of the statement takes on clarity. Humans can derive meaning from suffering. The pain of childbirth is endured because it is a purposeful pain, resulting in the emergence of a new person among us. The purposefulness of other suffering may be less dramatic, but it certainly includes its ability to spur us to empathize, to act compassionately, to learn how to improve our methods of relief, and to deepen our character through sharing in the suffering of others.

Those whose physical, psychological, or emotional pain is excruciating understandably want to be relieved of their suffering. Though we cannot fully comprehend what they are experiencing, our compassion compels us to seek the relief that they so desperately crave. Some have argued that euthanasia should be an option, while a few have even resorted to assisting in someone's suicide. Although the desire to relieve another's suffering is noble, if our thinking moves in the direction of euthanasia or assisted suicide, we must temper our compassion with humility. Our limited role in life's creation encourages a limited role in life's termination. It's a slippery slope of relativism we tread upon when we craft rationales to justify terminating someone's life. Without a consistent principle of life, today's well-intentioned exceptions can become tomorrow's base expectations.

Although no one wishes suffering on anyone, it comes to all of us to varying degrees throughout our lives. Some clearly suffer more than others. It's a mystery why, and any sane person would prefer to embrace the enjoyment of life and do without its pain. But despite our best efforts and therapies, the residual suffering that we are unable to relieve and must endure serves as a frustratingly sad but no less valuable opportunity to reflect on the complex dichotomy of life's joy and misery, pleasure and pain, light and darkness, good and bad. Since we can't completely avoid suffering, we must respond to it in ways that respect the suffering person as well as the person's suffering. We should offer to those who suffer our attentive presence, sustaining nutrition, physical comfort and effective pain relief. And for people of faith, we should also humbly pray that whatever mysterious purpose the suffering may serve, the person be relieved of it as quickly as possible. Moreover, we should be careful not to unintentionally engender the feeling that those who suffer have become a burden. Suffering is enough without the mental torment of feeling that they, or we, are less deserving of care.

But what of the argument about respecting someone's wish to die with dignity? Since oxygen, water, and nutrition are necessary to sustain human life from conception to death, their provision and acceptance are inherently dignified and natural. To deny them is cruel; to refuse them is self-destructive. However, highly sophisticated medical interventions are a different matter. Although we are morally obliged to offer them if available, no one is morally obligated to accept them. As stewards of our own lives, we have a choice, one that is preferably made before judgment is impaired by pain, medications, or coma. Our making this choice would wisely acknowledge life's limitations no less than its greatness, would provide guidance to those entrusted with our medical care, and would save our families the anguish of having to decide what level of intervention we would want for ourselves as we approach our bodily deaths. In looking at life naturally conceived, and seeing its corollary in death naturally entered, we accept sustaining nutrition but can, with a consistent principle of life, make the highly personal decision whether we wish to accept complex medical intervention.

ABORTION

Before Roe. v. Wade, an American woman who found herself unexpectedly pregnant, whether by failed family planning, relations outside of marriage, or as a result of rape, had several options. She could see the pregnancy through and raise the child herself, arrange for a family member to raise the child, or give the child up for adoption. She might have the option of entering into an otherwise ill-advised marriage. Or she could seek to abort the baby through self-inflicted actions or the services of an abortionist, either of which could, and often did, result in serious injury or death. The Roe v. Wade decision was believed to have enshrined in American law the right of a woman to solely decide whether to keep or abort a growing fetus up to a certain age without being subject to prosecution. It also paved the way for abortions to be performed by licensed doctors in sterile clinics and later by women taking FDA-approved abortifacients. This legal judgment gave women autonomy over their bodies, saved many from the butchery of unqualified practitioners, and enabled them to move on with their lives as if the unexpected pregnancy never happened – almost.

Although many women availed themselves of abortions one or even several times during their childbearing years, some report that on a deep, personal level, they have never shaken the belief that somehow what they did seemed right at the time but was nonetheless wrong. Some have anguished for years, most poignantly when they feel joy at the births of new children among family and friends, yet simultaneously feel regret over what might have been for them. We should honor such feelings, thoughts, and promptings of conscience.

Fewer men have had such misgivings. One of the consequences of Roe v. Wade was to 'liberate' men from even the minimal sense of responsibility society may have pressured them to assume in the past. Since abortion was legalized, our expectations of a man's responsibility have declined so much that today, a man is considered 'supportive' if he pays for a woman's abortion. Many do not even do that. Ironically, men are able to righteously declare their support for a woman while actually demonstrating even less support. Small wonder why many men are so 'enlightened' in their pro-abortion posture when it's in their self-interest to favor something that enables them to enjoy women carnally while absolving them of any responsibility.

The problem with Roe v. Wade seems to be three-fold. First, if the decision about the baby is framed as being the exclusive choice of the woman, then the man has neither rights nor responsibilities. It is left squarely on the shoulders of the woman, even more alone now than in the past, to contend with this unexpected state of affairs, the handling of which can have a profound impact upon her health, education, livelihood, and emotional well-being.

Second, it denies the legitimate parental interest of the man with whom the woman co-conceived the baby. Contrary to much of the discourse around abortion, some men are interested in and committed to raising their child regardless of the circumstances of the child's conception.

Third and most troubling, in deciding Roe v. Wade, the judges had to make an assumption about when human life begins. In their consideration of conception, the emergence of an embryo, and trimesters of fetal development, the judges had to identify a 'compelling point' during the nine-month human gestation period before which abortion would be allowed, but after which abortion would be prohibited. They couldn't concede life's genesis at conception; otherwise, abortion would amount to the killing of a person. But they couldn't decide life begins at birth because the baby is too obviously a baby. They also avoided the latter months of pregnancy because of what they described as the 'potentiality of human life' - what we lay people might ascertain as 'early stage development' from the fetus's very human characteristics inside the womb and ability to respond to stimuli outside the womb.

In the half-century since 1973's Roe v. Wade decision, our imaging equipment has become more sophisticated, providing us with an even earlier glimpse of a baby's development. Moreover, fetal viability has also changed, with earlier preemies having a greater chance of survival thanks to improvements in our medical technology and resources. The artificially constructed definition of human life's inception in the original legal decision, and subsequent developments in fetal healthcare, are enough to give many of those once in favor of abortion pause to reconsider whether the judges got it right in deciding Roe v. Wade.

In 2022, the U.S. Supreme Court decided quite differently by overturning the 1973 decision, declaring that the United States Constitution does not confer a right to abortion and that abortion is a matter to be decided by states and the voters in each state. A majority of American women were aghast, while a minority were pleased. The issue remains one of the most contentious in our country. It promises to become even more contentious because some states have begun to severely restrict abortion access, and in 2023, a federal court decided to limit an FDA-approved abortion pill, setting the stage for more court battles, protests, and political polarization.

No matter one's attitude toward abortion, it is not helpful - indeed, it is cruel - to make it more difficult for a woman to get an abortion. And what person, irrespective of gender, wants government to insert itself into highly personal, sensitive medical decisions? More constructive and dignity affirming would be to reduce the reasons why a woman would be put into a position to even consider abortion - the mother's health, fetal anomalies, not wanting to birth the child of a rapist, being too young to assume child rearing responsibilities, inadequate financial resources to raise a child, concern about bringing a child into an abusive relationship and myriad other reasons of a highly personal nature.

Notwithstanding the intelligence, integrity, and compassion of judges, they are fallible human beings. Judges have made decisions that, in retrospect, were ill advised. Consider the laws that once defined slaves as property to be treated as chattel by their owners. Their rationale was logically constructed, their decision was cogently argued, and they were able to identify societal 'benefits,' not the least of which was providing cheap labor to support an agrarian economy. In Nazi Germany, a legally constituted government singled out Jewish people, gypsies, homosexuals, the disabled, the infirm, and the insane to be systematically destroyed because they were considered less than fully human. Too few in Germany and elsewhere had the courage to balk. However, reluctantly, it was just accepted or ignored. Now we know better.

If you accept what many believe, that human life begins at conception, the implications of the 1973 decision are almost incomprehensible. It would mean acknowledging that Roe v. Wade ushered in a phase in American history when we made it legal to kill the most vulnerable among us. But is it reasonable to believe that human life begins at conception? No one has been able to prove 'metaphysically' when human life begins. In the 1973 Roe v. Wade decision, the judges chose a certain point during the typical nine-month pregnancy period as a matter of 'law.' Scientists have a variety of thoughtful theories and knowledgeable opinions but they are just that, theories and opinions, regardless of how strongly held. To put this in some historical context, and notwithstanding the incredible accomplishments resulting from the advancement of human knowledge, scientists don't always get it right at first. Earlier in history, the most learned once believed that the sun revolved around the earth, that the earth was flat, and even that smoking was good for you. Now, we know the contrary to be true. What we think to be a 'fact' one day can, and often does, change as we learn more. The legitimacy of policies, particularly controversial ones vigorously pursued without compromise, can, with additional time to reflect and evaluate, be seen in a completely different light, even by some of the original architects of those policies.

The Vietnam War of the 1960s is a case in point, with one of its primary architects, Defense Secretary Robert McNamara, having admitted many years later, in 1995, that American involvement was a mistake, one which cost over 58,000 Americans and over 3,000,000 Vietnamese their lives. So if the most powerful decision makers, most respected judges, and best trained scientists can make assumptions that subsequently prove to be flawed, perhaps those who believe that life begins at conception are not so unreasonable after all.

But we needn't rely upon society's elite to make distinctions about the flesh-and-blood matters of life. We have our own intuition. For example, we recoil with antipathy at animals that kill their offspring. Yet we humans secured legal sanction to kill our own species. And it wasn't just women. It was all of us – men and women alike - who bought into the argument and accepted the decision to legalize abortion as a means to ameliorate the harm then endured by many unexpectedly pregnant women.

No one wants to see women put into the hands of incompetent abortionists, relegated to filthy underground clinics, consume unsafe drugs, or be forced to raise children conceived in rape. But in our search for a resolution to the problem of unplanned pregnancies, we err profoundly in seeking our answer in the slaughter of innocents, whether with or without federal or state sanction. If we wish to create a culture that truly honors life – including that of an unborn child, a pregnant woman, and a biological father – we need to accomplish five substantial changes in American society.

FIRST, we need to acknowledge the consequences of 1973's Roe v. Wade decision. If we are to accept the profound implications of having terminated untold numbers of unborn children during their early stage of development, we need to demonstrate compassion, understanding, and forgiveness on a scale never attempted in American society. The guilt that could be unleashed could have a deleterious effect on the emotional health of millions of women as well as men. But guilt's relief through forgiveness could be immensely therapeutic in absolving us for what we have done, and failed to do, under abortion's government sanction. Neither now nor ever will there be a time for judgment, accusations, or retribution whether someone initiated an act of abortion, supported its accomplishment, or simply looked the other way.

SECOND, we must give the unexpectedly pregnant woman or girl far more institutional, as well as individual, support to exercise other options, such as raising the child herself, entrusting her baby with family members, or offering the baby to loving adoptive couples. That means we have to allocate appropriate levels of public funding, streamline adoption procedures, and make adjustments in our educational institutions and places of employment to accommodate women carrying their babies full term. Unlike in the past, society must deliver consistent, comprehensive, and tangible support to unexpectedly pregnant women and girls. Respect, rather than shame, should accompany each pregnant person irrespective of marital status. Through the sacrifices she is making to carry a baby to full term she is honoring life. As a civilized society, we owe her no less than our full support – spoken and substantive.

THIRD, our law enforcement and judicial systems must take a harder line on rape. It is such a gross personal violation and so emotionally harmful to the victim and her relationships that society cannot continue to treat rape with the level of suspicion we still too often see. Prosecution of rapists should be swift, incarceration of those fairly convicted severe, and for serial sex offenders, administration of chemical castration drugs imposed. Considering that rape is often perpetrated by people

131

known by the victim, we could provide a powerful preventative to discourage rape via a court ordered requirement that any man who is proven by DNA testing to have raped a woman would be responsible for child support until the child turns twenty years of age. That should make a lot of men think twice before forcing themselves on a woman. And for society overall, those in positions of influence within organizations or online must do a better job of inculcating respect for women's reproductive sexuality, especially our storytellers, who could be more temperate in portraying violence in movies, TV programs, videos, and online games.

FOURTH, we must do a better job of educating about the power of sex to change lives. Sex education cannot be limited to discussions about sexually transmitted diseases, but must be more holistic, encompassing the physical, psychological, emotional, and spiritual dimensions of our sexuality. Parents, schools, youth organizations, places of worship, and accredited online learning platforms need to become more actively engaged in the moral development of our citizens. It is not enough to simply encourage abstinence outside of marriage, and family planning within marriage, however useful those lessons may be. We must embrace our sexually budding youth where they live their lives in what has become a hyper sexualized 21st century culture. We would be well advised to also remind our adults that there are consequences to engaging in sex irresponsibly. Much as we may like to fantasize about having sex without consequence, we can't, in fact. It's like expecting to be able to repeatedly pig out on our favorite foods without gaining weight. If we overeat, we run the risk of obesity, heart disease, and a host of other ailments. If we engage in sexual relations indiscriminately, we run the risk of transmitting disease, disassociating sex from affection, and unintentionally conceiving a new human life. There are certain natural laws that govern our existence, and we ignore them at our own peril.

FIFTH, as a democratic society with constitutional protections for individual liberty, we are compelled to accept that we cannot impose restrictive sexual practices upon those who do not share certain beliefs. Not everyone finds the argument against artificial contraception sufficiently compelling to alter behavior. Their beliefs about the purpose and meaning of sexual relations are matters for their conscience and the God whom they may worship. For those who believe that every act of sexual intercourse need not be open to the possibility of creating new life, then contraception is a legitimate option to preclude the unintended generation of new life. Irrespective of religious convictions, or lack thereof, most of us have within us the power to initiate the conception and nurture the development of new persons – a power warranting self-respect, mutual respect, and wise stewardship of that power if we are to consistently honor life.

If we accomplish the aforementioned five suggested societal changes - (i) no longer judging women's private medical decisions; (ii) providing substantive, sustained support to pregnant women; (iii) holding men responsible for the consequences of their behavior; (iv) providing authentically comprehensive sex education at puberty; and (v) respecting personal contraception decisions - then the circumstances in which a woman would find herself even needing to contemplate abortion would be profoundly reduced in our society. Over time, this would leave far fewer situations where a woman or girl would need to resort to abortion, always a decision best left to the woman and her family in consultation with her physician.

CONCLUDING COMMENTS

As we ponder the awesomeness of human life and consider our mutual dependence to help each other throughout life, our thoughts necessarily turn from the philosophical to the practical in determining what type of society we wish to create. Do we want to become accustomed to the pre-meditated taking of people's lives? Are we prepared to acknowledge our limited role in life's creation and equally prepared to accept a limited role in life's termination? Are we ready to recognize men's and women's equal rights as well as responsibilities? Can we learn from past flawed judgments that it is always wrong to rationalize a lesser value of some people's lives? Can we respect the private nature of medical decisions and not insert government dictates into the doctor patient relationship?

We have decades of experience demonstrating our ability to violate a consistent principle of life by killing prisoners we abhor, terminating those whose suffering we're unable to relieve, and aborting those whom we've defined as shy of full personhood. Isn't it time for us to transform our society with a higher level of civility in which we send an unambiguous message that every person has value? In this regard our task is a simple one - to respect life wherever we may find it.

What We Can Do

It is incumbent upon all citizens to become informed about the critical issues facing our nation and our communities. With our rights come responsibilities, not the least of which is making informed choices at the ballot box. To help in this regard, below is a Candidate Evaluation checklist which you can use to evaluate politicians campaigning for your vote to hold public office. Assess them yourself and decide which candidate is best prepared and most likely to take a transpartisan common sense approach to creating a culture of life.

Candidate Evaluation Criteria

	Candidate _____'s Position on Creating a Culture of Life	Yes/No
1	Allows women and doctors fully informed healthcare choices without fear of liability	
2	Supports widely advertised and available alternatives to abortion	
3	Encourages age appropriate comprehensive sex education and access to contraception	
4	Favors highly restrictive lifetime imprisonment as an alternative to capital punishment	
5	Supports making inmates work to help compensate for the cost of their incarceration	
6	Funds expanded availability of hospice care and pain medications for the terminally ill	

The information, data and statistics mentioned came from a wide variety of open sources available over the internet. A debt of gratitude is expressed for the hard work of all those people at so many different private and public sector organizations who spend countless hours collecting and collating data, researching information, verifying facts, and producing reports for public consumption, which profoundly facilitates the creation of an informed citizenry upon which our democracy depends. Among those sources:

ThePublicDiscourse.com

Pursuing a Foreign Policy of Global Leadership

Being Smart, Strong and Strategic

According to historians, over the past 3,400 years of recorded history, humans have been at war - defined as conflicts in which more than 1,000 lives have been lost - 92% of the time, enjoying peace during just 268 of those 3,400 years. That's pathetic; only 8% of the time that our world has been at peace. In just the twentieth century alone, over 100 million people have been killed in wars. Over the entire course of human history, scholars estimate that up to 1 billion people have been killed in wars. Our world is a dangerous place; it always has been and always will be - at least until the second coming of Christ.

Consequently, our foreign policy must first be based upon the sober reality of how the world actually operates, not based upon naïve assumptions, ideological biases, fact-denying histories, or politically convenient narratives. Only when we are grounded in objective facts can we logically craft realistic foreign policies infused with common sense ideas that acknowledge the challenges that reality imposes, while also incorporating our aspirations for a better, more peaceful, and prosperous world that values human life, personal dignity, and individual freedom. We cannot afford to err on the side of starting with aspirations that fail to account for the harsh real world context in which foreign policies must be developed and executed. It serves no one who is genuinely interested in peace to spout appealing idealistic rhetoric which fails to take into account an accurate and comprehensive understanding of history, missed opportunities, challenges, threats, and the disingenuousness of certain players on the world stage.

136

When it comes to the breadth of a government's policies, the stakes could not be higher, nor the results more consequential, than with its foreign policy. Indeed, there is arguably no greater existential threat to a nation than an ill-conceived or poorly executed foreign policy. In this regard, crafting our foreign policy must start with 'realpolitik' - the real time facts and circumstances of the world - and proceed to incorporate our realizable strategic objectives, in accordance with our moral and ethical values.

Under the United States Constitution, the President establishes what our country's foreign policy shall be, with the advice of the Secretary of State and the consent of the U.S. Senate. In practice, the President receives information and advice from his National Security Council (NSC), established in 1947 and comprised of the National Security Advisor, Chairman of the Joint Chiefs of Staff, Director of National Intelligence, Secretary of State, Secretary of Defense, Secretary of Homeland Security, Secretary of the Treasury, Secretary of Energy, Attorney General, Vice President, Ambassador to the United Nations, Administrator of the U.S. Agency for International Development, Chief of Staff to the President, Assistant to the President for National Security Affairs, Counsel to the President, Legal Advisor to the NSC and other senior officials as needed, such as when addressing issues around public health, cyber security, migration, climate, etc.

The three primary goals of U.S. foreign policy are to protect the United States and its interests around the world, which include unfettered access to international resources and markets, to preserve a peaceful balance of power in the world, and to advance human rights and democracy. Although the goals are clear, actually crafting and implementing foreign policy is a complex endeavor because it is a dynamic process which necessarily requires constant adjusting as regional and global circumstances change.

Generally speaking, we have three types of tools in our foreign policy toolkit - economic, humanitarian, and military. Our favored method of using our tools to influence the decisions of other governments and the behavior of other countries is through diplomacy - communication, negotiation, relationship building, and promotion of mutual interests. The objective of the diplomatic element of our foreign policy is to talk, meet, negotiate, and make agreements in order to align interests or solve problems before they may metastasize into conflicts that necessitate the use of military force.

Just in our own lifetime, we have seen a decades long Cold War end, followed by a hopeful thaw in relations with the former Soviet Union, only to subsequently see new leadership in Russia launch a hot war against the newly democratic independent European nation of Ukraine. This was unimaginable to virtually everyone, including me as a tourist in Kyiv in 2004 enjoying the culture, cuisine, and company of Ukrainians, as well as in Moscow strolling through Red Square, touring the Kremlin, visiting a military museum, and attending the Bolshoi Ballet, in what at the time seemed like a new era of warm, friendly relations. Twenty years later, we find that Russia's hot war in Europe has reinstated a Cold War with the entire West and necessitated the strengthening and expansion of NATO amidst concerns about more Russian aggression.

On the positive side, foreign policies can also be beneficially transformative, even to the point where a country that was once an enemy can later become a friend, even an ally. World War II provides remarkable examples of how Germany and Japan once fought the United States in bitter conflicts, but after the wars ended, the United States crafted brilliant, common sense foreign polices that facilitated these countries becoming democracies and transforming into some of our closest freedom loving, economically advanced, peaceful allies.

Given the complexities, volatility, and dangers of our world, made especially so in our lifetime by the current aggressive foreign policies and military activities of such powerful nations as Russia, China, North Korea, and Iran, it has been and remains imperative that the United States maintain a strong national defense, reliable treaty relationships with allies, a consistent influential role in multinational institutions and globally projectable military capability second to none. By being strong, smart, and strategic, we can best proactively deter aggressor nations from launching hostile actions and respond to them most effectively when they do.

With the dissolution of the U.S.S.R. in 1991 and the end of the Cold War, the United States was left as the sole superpower and eagerly, if perhaps naively, anticipated democracy emerging within its former greatest adversary, hoping that many of its republics would transform into independent democracies. This happened with several Eastern European countries, such as Romania, where my wife and I, vacationing there in 2006, could feel the excitement among Bucharest residents about their country's impending 2007 membership in the European Union. Several other countries in the former Soviet sphere of influence became independent, but some democratic in name only, retaining strong ties to, and often doing the bidding of, Russia. Sadly, many of our initial post-Cold War optimistic expectations were short lived.

There is no better example than Ukraine, which became an independent state in 1991, but remained governed by pro-Russian presidents. By 2014, Ukrainians' desire to no longer be controlled by Moscow and to reorient itself toward the West led to mass protests and a revolution that resulted in the pro-Russian president fleeing to Moscow. Russia reacted by sending troops into Ukraine's Crimea, where they took over government buildings and infrastructure and eventually annexed the peninsula. Russia also backed supposed 'separatists' in Ukraine's eastern Donbas region and later proclaimed independent republics of Donetsk and Luhansk, eventually annexing them as well. The Minsk II Agreement

139

between Ukraine and Russia was signed in 2015, but never fully implemented, leading to a static conflict - until 2022 when Russia bombed and invaded Ukraine on the orders of President Vladimir Putin, who not only authorized the indiscriminate killing of innocent men, women and children, but also outrageously questioned Ukraine's right to exist.

The invasion was internationally condemned, and the United States, Canada, Europe, and dozens of countries came to the aid of Ukraine, providing military, intelligence, and economic assistance and welcoming Ukrainian elderly, women, and child refugees. As of this writing, the war continues to grind on, with Russia showing no mercy in its indiscriminate bombing of residences, schools, theaters, hospitals, electrical grids, and other non-military targets. Having visited Ukraine several times, walking the beautiful boulevards of Kyiv, taking in the rich cultural heritage in its museums and theaters, and enjoying the graciousness and warmth of its people, it is heartbreaking to me, and devastating to my wife, who grew up and went to college in Kyiv, to see the death and destruction unleashed upon Ukrainians and their beloved country.

Thanks to the coalition of democracies that aligned to help Ukraine defend itself, Ukraine is also managing to degrade Russia's military capabilities and, as the first line of defense, protect the rest of Europe from further Russian encroachment. Were that encroachment to happen, it would trigger NATO's collective defense provisions that would bring the nuclear-weapons-capable United States into direct conflict with the comparably nuclear-equipped Russia, a prospect that would have unimaginably catastrophic consequences.

This brings us to another essential element of crafting sensible foreign policies - alliances and partnerships. Perhaps the most recognizable treaty alliance is the aforementioned NATO - the North Atlantic Treaty Organization - an intergovernmental military alliance founded in 1949 and currently comprised of 31 member states, 29 European and two North American. NATO guarantees the security of its members through political and military cooperation, the former by promoting democratic values and mutual trust, and the latter through collective defense.

There has always been a strain in foreign policy thinking among 'isolationist' Americans who believe that we should not get involved in world affairs. Thankfully, in the lead up to World War II, their naïve thinking was not persuasive, which enabled the United States to help Europe successfully defend itself against the spread of fascism and nazism. It is hard to imagine what Europe, indeed the world, would look like today if the United Kingdom, France, Italy, and the rest of Europe had fallen into the hands of totalitarian governments. America would likely not have long survived in its current form if the entirety of a totalitarian and militarized Europe became our enemy.

Former President Ronald Reagan eloquently spoke about this in his 1984 tribute to 'the boys of Pointe du Hoc,' during the commemoration of the 40th anniversary of the Normandy Invasion, D-Day: *"We in America have learned bitter lessons from two World Wars: It is better to be here ready to protect the peace, than to take blind shelter across the sea, rushing to respond only after freedom is lost. We've learned that isolationism never was and never will be an acceptable response to tyrannical governments with an expansionist intent."*

Unfortunately, today, we still have some isolationist politicians questioning the value of NATO and foolishly suggesting that the United States withdraw from NATO, reflecting a profound ignorance of history and the importance of such an essential common defense alliance in our dangerous world.

America is "the indispensable nation," as noted by Madeleine Albright, our 64th, and first female, Secretary of State. American leadership is indeed indispensable on the world stage. Unlike the isolationists who would have America retreat from its role on the world stage and let belligerent nations project their malign influence around the globe, Americans must remain engaged internationally and lead with honorable commitments, backed by reliable actions, which friendly nations can rely upon and hostile nations can fear.

No other democracy has the military might, economic power, and cultural influence to act as a bulwark against the forces that seek to replace democracy with various forms of authoritarianism, which muzzles the press, imprisons political opponents, oppresses citizens, denigrates human rights, disrespects international borders and dismisses other nations' territorial integrity. However, given the growing economic and especially military might of certain adversaries, the United States cannot act as an effective bulwark alone. We need alliances to act as a deterrent, and, when that fails, to push back against aggression.

So NATO, as well as other treaty alliances, such as the North American Defense Command with Canada known as NORAD, the Indo-Pacific region tri-lateral security partnership among the United States, United Kingdom and Australia known as AUKUS, the anglosphere intelligence sharing agreement among the United States, United Kingdom, Canada, Australia and New Zealand known as Five Eyes, shorthand for AUS/CAN/NZ/UK/US EYES ONLY, are integral parts of America's foreign policy. While military and intelligence sharing treaties get the most public attention, it should be noted that treaties are also used to set international boundaries, trade rules, postal protocols, and, increasingly, environmental protections. A rules-based world order benefits everyone interested in peace and prosperity, but is despised by dictators who wish to reorder the world to achieve their malevolent aims.

Less formal, and typically shorter in duration, are 'partnerships' which develop mutually beneficial relationships between countries. For example, the State Partnership Program organizes U.S. National Guard Units to partner with foreign militaries to learn from each other. Partnerships are also used for information exchanges, collaboration on infrastructure projects, joint efforts to interdict drug traffickers, share cultural experiences, fight cyber criminals, etc. Some partnerships are humanitarian in nature. The annual Pacific Partnership sees the U.S. Navy dispatch one of its two hospital ships to countries in the Indo-Pacific region. While in port in such countries as Bangladesh or Indonesia, its crew and skilled passengers provide medical care to poor residents and assist with infrastructure projects, such as repairing schools and building hospitals. These partnership activities generate goodwill and enhance our influence as a force for good around the world.

Of growing usefulness in foreign policy is the advancement of public-private partnerships, which leverage the resources and expertise resident within private sector organizations to achieve government objectives, such as building infrastructure, promoting investment, and encouraging trade, which can develop a country's economy, improve living standards and build closer ties between nations.

Finally, if we have learned anything from the plethora of disinformation and misleading narratives that spread across the internet negatively influencing citizens, it is that a democratic nation's foreign policy must be communicated in a clear, correct, and concise manner domestically as well as internationally, particularly when lives are in harm's way. We need to look no further than the recent Israel-Hamas War to see how critical it is to provide people near and far with correct information to understand the rationale for why a particular policy is adopted and implemented. This tragic war provides a stark example of how a lack of understanding of history, circulation of provocative imagery without correct contextual information, ideological intransigence, and willful ignorance can converge to create emotionally charged misunderstandings that lead to political divisiveness, misdirected protestations and resort to violence.

Conflicts are often complex, full of gray areas that don't lend themselves to simple black-and-white narratives. A tragic example with which the world is currently grappling is in the Middle East. We know that Hamas is committed to the destruction of Israel. It's in their organization's founding documents, and their leaders publicly state that they will continue October 7th type attacks again and again. Like any country, Israel has a right to defend itself. But we also know that most Palestinians are not terrorists and simply want to live their lives as best as they can in the impoverished Gaza Strip and the West Bank.

The complexities in objectively understanding the Israeli-Palestinian conflict arise because: (a) Hamas spent billions of foreign aid dollars building tunnels and acquiring weapons and rockets to attack Israel, money that could have been used to improve the quality of life of Gazans; (b) Hamas embeds its fighters within the civilian population, knowingly making innocent men, women and children human shields with their lives at risk whenever Israel predictably tries to eradicate Hamas terrorists in response to an attack; (c) the carnage of innocent Israeli and Palestinian lives lost is gut-wrenching and understandably prompts anger and protestations on both sides of the conflict; (d) Israel is prosecuting a war in a dense urban environment which inevitably generates a horrific amount of 'collateral damage' which has garnered widespread international condemnation; (e) there is currently no consensus among any regional players as to who will secure and govern Gaza after the fighting stops; and (f) there remains tremendous future uncertainly in the larger regional context of nuclear weapons aspiring Shia-Muslim Iran, backer of Hamas, Hezbollah and other terrorist groups and whom some speculate authorized the October 7th attack to derail the anticipated peace deal between the State of Israel and Iran's regional competitor, Sunni-Muslim Saudi Arabia. Complex indeed.

Multiple layered dimensions and dynamically changing uncertainties do not lend themselves to simple narratives. Nor do they lend themselves to easy resolution of this current conflict, nor of defusing generations long distrust and animosity, now presumably prolonged for additional future generations. While not all international conflicts are as layered as this particular one, they all do share one thing in common - the need to provide people near and far with a comprehensive understanding of the issues underlying the conflict so that observers' assessments will be based upon rationality more than emotions.

While a big picture understanding of our country's foreign policy should be part of every American citizen's basic civic awareness, when a particular U.S. foreign policy rises to the level of controversy, the level of information dissemination should be increased accordingly, commensurate with the gravity and urgency of the particular policy. This will help to ensure that people are correctly informed to facilitate their continued support and that outside observers have an accurate understanding of the reasons for our country's actions around the world.

The importance of the U.S. pursuing a common sense foreign policy of global leadership cannot be underestimated. In our intelligence agencies' most recent Annual Threat Assessment, reported by the Director of National Intelligence in February 2024, we read: *"The United States faces an increasingly fragile global order strained by accelerating strategic competition among major powers, more intense and unpredictable transnational challenges, and multiple regional conflicts with far-reaching implications."* Their report describes the challenges that U.S. foreign policy makers face: *"Regional and localized conflicts and instability ... will demand U.S. attention as states and non-state actors struggle in this evolving global order, including over major power competition and shared transnational challenges."*

145

At his inauguration in 1961, President John F. Kennedy addressed his international audience with words reflective of America's leadership role, "*My fellow citizens of the world: ask not what America will do for you, but what together we can do for the freedom of man.*"

Every generation of Americans has believed, millions have fought for and far too many have died defending America as a force for good on the world stage, a legacy which each new generation of Americans needs to continue. Though the circumstances and challenges may change over time, the indispensable role that America plays on the world stage should not be allowed to diminish lest our country and the world be put in great peril.

So, it is suggested that our development of a sensible foreign policy should be premised upon a critical combination of: (i) a sober 'realpolitik' understanding of our world as it is; (ii) advanced and sustained military prowess second to none; (iii) consistent and reliable American engagement globally; (iv) strong and durable multilateral alliances and mutually beneficial partnerships; (v) advancement of purposeful public-private partnerships; and (vi) effective domestic and international communications protocols.

Together, these six elements form the foundation of a common sense foreign policy structure that serves as both our and our allies' best defense, as well as the most effective antidote to the forces throughout our broken world which work against stability and peace, which disregard human dignity and freedom, which preclude economic opportunity, which stifle personal aspirations and which erode the quality of life for millions of individuals and families. Therefore, any politician aspiring to national public office should be willing to explain the basis upon which they would develop and support the foreign policies of the United States.

What We Can Do

It is incumbent upon all citizens to become informed about the critical issues facing our nation and our communities. With our rights come responsibilities, not the least of which is making informed choices at the ballot box. To help in this regard, below is a Candidate Evaluation Criteria checklist which you can use to evaluate one politician as compared to another politician campaigning for your vote to hold public office. Assess them yourself and decide which candidate is best prepared and most likely to take a **transpartisan** common sense approach to foreign affairs.

Candidate Evaluation Criteria

	Candidate _____'s Position on Foreign Policy	Yes/No
1	Has a solid understanding of history and international relations	
2	Supports a strong military with the ability to project power globally	
3	Seeks to advance international relations through robust diplomacy	
4	Endeavors to strengthen and expand alliance relationships like NATO and others	
5	Advances U.S. leadership at the United Nations and at multilateral institutions like the International Monetary Fund and World Bank	
6	Fosters public-private partnerships to advance our foreign policy objectives.	
7	Encourages civic education and communication about our foreign policies	

The information, data and statistics mentioned came from a wide variety of open sources available over the internet. A debt of gratitude is expressed for the hard work of all those people at so many different private and public sector organizations who spend countless hours collecting and collating data, researching information, verifying facts, and producing reports for public consumption, which profoundly facilitates the creation of an informed citizenry upon which our democracy depends. Among those sources:

Wikipedia

Britannica.com

Department of Defense

Foreign Affairs

History.com

History.Army.mil

History.State.gov

HistoryOfWar.org

Library of Congress

Office of the U.S. Trade Representative

OurWorldInData.org

NYTimes.com Best Books of 2023, "What Every Person Should Know About War" by Chris Hedges

The World Bank

The Hill, "Our Unraveling World Is History Repeating Itself" by Robert Manning

Annual Threat Assessment, February 5, 2024, Director of National Intelligence

Thriving in the Land of Opportunity

Advancing Civic and Personal Responsibility

Based upon a 17,000 person survey soliciting perceptions about 87 nations as reported in a 2023 article in U.S. News and World Report, the United States is perceived overall to be the 5th best country in the world, behind Switzerland, Canada, Sweden, and Australia. We came in 4th for perceptions of being the most tech-savvy, innovative, trendy, fashionable, having a good legal framework, and significance in entertainment. We took 3rd place as perceived for the best country to start a career, our digital infrastructure, a good job market, being progressive, having strong exports and cultural influence. We garnered 2nd perceived place for being connected to the rest of the world, being a leader, politically influential, modern, economically influential, having well developed infrastructure, a strong military, being the best country to invest in, and best country for studying abroad. We aced the 1st perceived position in agility, power, most forward-looking country, best country for education, most influential, most dynamic, strong international alliances, easy access to capital, strong consumer brands, and being the most entrepreneurial.

Reflective of these perceptions, as well as individuals' particular reasons, the United States has been the primary destination of choice for international migrants since 1970, according to the 2022 World Migration Report. Of all the people legally immigrating to the United States in 2021, the vast majority, nearly three-quarters, came for employment or education - 42% for work, 32% for school, 23% for family reunification, and 3% for other reasons - according to USAFacts.org. People - native born and immigrants alike - know that if you learn and work hard, you can get ahead in

America. There may be obstacles and inequities along the way, and admittedly, we have a legacy of slavery and residual racism and prejudice to overcome, but few countries compare for the breadth of opportunities for advancement afforded individuals who have a strong work ethic and persevere in applying their talents and energies. And for those innovative thinking individuals with a brilliant idea and entrepreneurship skills, the United States is the venue of choice to launch a business and sell into a large and dynamic market.

Being the land of opportunity does not happen spontaneously, of course. There are arguably at least five cultural prerequisites for the land of opportunity to broadly benefit its residents: (i) strong work ethic; (ii) playing by the rules; (iii) nation of laws; (iv) judging behavior, not appearance; and (v) shared moral values.

STRONG WORK ETHIC

For generations, we have seen that a strong work ethic lifts individuals and their families from poverty to dignified standards of living, improving themselves and influencing generations that follow to apply that strong work ethic to their chosen fields of endeavor. Naturally, not everyone succeeds to the same degree. There is no equality of result. America, or any country for that matter, can only aspire to offer equality of opportunity, and that, we know, has historically been offered more equitably to some than to others. Our young nation is a work in progress, and though we still have a long way to go to achieve that often quoted "more perfect Union" mentioned in the Preamble of the U.S. Constitution, we have already achieved tremendous progress and are poised to make more remarkable progress - if we honestly and courageously confront our challenges, including an unintended socio-economic trend that has emerged in modern American society challenging the value of a strong work ethic. But first, a bit of history is in order.

151

Prior to the Great Depression that began in 1929, anti-poverty programs were largely the responsibility of private sector charities or state or local governments, but these organizations were overwhelmed by the depth and breadth of human needs created during the Great Depression. Franklin D. Roosevelt's 1935 New Deal included the creation of Aid to Families with Dependent Children, geared primarily toward families with children and widowed mothers. The New Deal's Work Projects Administration (WPA), also created in 1935, was oriented toward employing primarily men in infrastructure and construction building projects. These programs were conceived to provide economic assistance to the unemployed and financially struggling families. In the 1960s came the emergence of the modern welfare system with the passage of the Public Welfare Amendments to expand public assistance and improve child welfare services, which now includes, Medicaid, Supplemental Security Income, Supplemental Nutrition Assistance Program, Children's Health Insurance Program, Temporary Assistance for Needy Families, Housing Assistance and the Earned Income Tax Credit.

Successive federal administrations have tried to make adjustments to the various public assistance programs, especially to incentivize work but without penalties, and to shift more program control to individual states to enable them to be more flexible in administering the programs based upon actual needs. The landmark Personal Responsibility and Work Opportunity Reconciliation Act of 1996 (PRWORA) was a bi-partisan effort in this regard, part of the Republican Party's 'Contract with America' and Democratic President Bill Clinton's promise to *'end welfare as we know it,'* which implemented significant changes to U.S. social welfare policy. It focused on welfare dependency, out-of-wedlock births, and multigenerational poverty. It attempted to end welfare as an entitlement and instead required recipients to begin working after two years of benefits, placed a five year lifetime limit on federally funded benefits, discouraged out-of-wedlock births, enhanced enforcement of child support, and restricted funding to immigrants. Many states pitched the programmatic changes as 'welfare to work' programs.

The well-intentioned policy changes had mixed results. Some declared that the legislation's effectiveness in reducing welfare was a success. From 1997 to 2000, there was a 53% drop in total recipients from having left, or been terminated from, welfare. However, although the number of welfare caseloads declined by 56%, there was recorded only a 1% decline in the poverty rate. And the number of children living in extreme poverty, defined as household income below 50% of the poverty level, actually increased.

According to the Center on Budget and Policy Priorities, work requirements did not reduce poverty as anticipated. Increased employment weakened over time and stable employment proved elusive for many recipients. Indeed, most recipients were not better off, and some sank deeper into poverty. These results, contrary to expectations, proved especially true for women who, without proper education and training, and bearing primary child rearing responsibilities, were unable to secure adequately compensatory jobs to sustain themselves and their children, nor to access affordable child care. This was not inconsequential considering that, according to the National Women's Law Center, over 10 million women were the sole support for their children and families.

PRWORA also shifted responsibility for services from the federal government to state governments, and authorized each state to make its own rules, sometimes more restrictive, regarding how people could access services and to determine how much federal money would be directed to social safety net programs within their state. These changes led to increased inequality among 50 state programs.

With the tech bubble crash recession of 2001, and the housing bubble and financial markets meltdown of 2008, came increased unemployment, greater child poverty, and more single parent households below the poverty limit.

Let's look at just one of the most essential welfare benefit programs for the poor - the Supplemental Nutrition Assistance Program (SNAP), which provides food benefits to low income families to supplement their grocery budget. According to the U.S. Census Bureau, in 2021, approximately 55% of Americans in poverty were women, and 33% of households receiving SNAP benefits were headed by a female without a spouse. According to the Government Accountability Office, 51% of adults receiving SNAP benefits work at least 35 hours per week for most of the year. According to the Bureau of Labor Statistics, women are 20% more likely than men to be among the working poor. Contrary to popular perceptions among some, according to the U.S. Department of Agriculture (USDA), data from 2020 indicates that white Americans represented the largest group of SNAP benefit recipients at 38.4%, black Americans 28.4%, Hispanic Americans 11.8%, Asian Americans 2.4%, Native Americans 1.5% and others 17.5%.

Two socio-economic facts stand out: half the people receiving SNAP benefits are working, but their jobs, primarily in the service sector, are so low skilled and low paying that their incomes are insufficient to adequately feed themselves and their families; and far more women than men experience poverty and, therefore, become dependent upon these benefits. This reflects several ongoing challenges that we still face as a society: (i) we need to do a better job of encouraging and providing education and skills development that qualify people for better than poverty level wage jobs; (ii) we need to better instill a strong work ethic among our youth to put them on a better life trajectory than welfare dependency; (iii) we need to improve our provision of the support that women need, including access to affordable childcare; and (iv) we need to hold 'baby fathers' financially responsible for the costs of raising their children, whether conceived in or out of wedlock.

As a society, we know that babies need nourishment. Mothers need support to be good mothers. Boys and girls need resources to support learning and character development. Adults need vocational or professional training and opportunities to apply their talents and skills to earn a living. Seniors on limited incomes need assistance with food, medical expenses, housing, and elder care. Practically and morally, our society is right to offer benefits for the wellbeing of those who truly need them, while also encouraging development of a strong work ethic and personal responsibility to enhance self-reliance and limit dependence upon society's welfare benefits.

PLAYING BY THE RULES

As we go about addressing the aforementioned challenges, we must acknowledge that a portion of the people receiving welfare benefits are not genuinely in need and are gaming the system. They have learned what to say to social services case workers, what to put on benefits applications, what information to withhold from agencies, etc., in order to navigate through welfare system eligibility criteria and secure benefits. Some are clever enough to avoid having bank accounts that social services can check to see how much money an applicant may have and instead only use check cashing services which typically cannot be traced. Newer online financial apps can also facilitate the hiding of financial resources from traditional verification systems.

But it's not just some welfare recipients who sometimes don't play by the rules. Within our local communities, who among us hasn't seen cars with obscured license plates so that toll cameras are unable to read their plate numbers, thereby evading payment for driving over public infrastructure? Or high profile individuals who commit fraud of various types to avoid paying their fair share of civil society's costs. And individuals are not unique in cheating the government.

Corporations sometimes disingenuously exploit loopholes, misrepresent information, manipulate their tax liability, evade regulations, or unfairly gain competitive advantage. Some arrange their operations in such a way as to receive subsidies from the government when they would otherwise still invest in certain business activities. Cheating is ubiquitous. It's part of the human condition, and all too often, the cost of monitoring, auditing, and prosecuting cheaters can be prohibitively expensive. It's sad but true that some of our fellow citizens are dishonest, and the rest of us have to pay for their cheating.

People learn from what they have been exposed to, particularly from the behavior of the adults in their families and communities. If a child observes their parents getting up each morning, taking care of household responsibilities, and going to work in order to pay for their home and to buy the food, clothing, and other household items that the family needs, chances are that child is going to replicate some or all of those positive behaviors when they grow up. On the other hand, if a child observes their parents - or just one parent and often unmarried - sleeping late, not going to a job to earn a living, not going to school to improve themselves, not being productive at home, but instead for years just going to the local welfare office to claim benefits from the government, chances are that child is not going to develop a strong work ethic and may develop a welfare ethic. How can we expect our fellow citizens to improve themselves through education, earn a living from working at a job, save for future needs, and act with self-agency as opposed to looking to a welfare agency, if those behaviors aren't observed in the authority figures within their families and neighborhoods? Even worse, in some communities, some adolescents grow up observing that the people with the money, fashionable clothes, flashy cars, etc., are the criminals who sell drugs, act as pimps, trade in illegal guns, engage in smash-and-grab store theft to sell stolen goods on online platforms, attack and rob their fellow citizens or stalk and shoot other gang members competing in criminal economic activities.

Children take in what they experience, and adolescents are astute observers of how one gets ahead in life. If they observe honesty, compassion, diligent study, and hard work among their elders, they are more likely to develop self-esteem, self-respect, self-reliance, and self-discipline and to grow into thriving members of their communities. If they observe neglect, dishonesty, cruelty, laziness, cheating the system, and criminality, they are more likely to become self-loathing, jealous, miserable adults expending their energies on negative, even harmful, activities and becoming a menace in their communities and a burden on society.

Sadly, we have places in our society where the latter is more prevalent than the former. If we are going to be honest with ourselves, we must ask, who among us - had we not had respectable upbringings by responsible parents, observed positive adult role models, attended well resourced schools with engaged teachers, lived and played in safe neighborhoods, etc. - would not have grown up to be less than stellar citizens, resorting to whatever means is necessary to survive? It should not be surprising that many people, across multiple generations, having grown up under dignity-destroying circumstances, developed a welfare ethic rather than a work ethic.

Concern about multigenerational dependency on public welfare benefits has existed for decades. As alluded to earlier, numerous efforts to encourage recipients to get off welfare have had mixed results. In fairness to those receiving public assistance who desired to get off assistance, taking a job might result in losing food, housing, and other financial benefits and Medicaid health coverage, as well as in incurring prohibitively expensive job related costs, such as for transportation and child care. Most welfare recipients are smart enough to do the math. The eligibility criteria sometimes serve as a disincentive to

157

getting a job since the compensation package of the typically low wage jobs that welfare recipients might be eligible for won't match their combined public assistance benefits.

Our welfare laws and regulations need to be adjusted to achieve four compelling improvements in playing by the rules: (i) provide common sense eligibility requirements that identify legitimate needs, including for childcare responsibilities that primarily fall to women; (ii) adopt a far more flexible and finely tuned sliding scale of benefit eligibility to not inadvertently disincentivize work; (iii) hold fathers financially and practically responsible for their children's rearing and education through age 20, the failure for which would subject these men to prosecution; and (iv) provide experiential training in developing self-reliance and self-discipline, as well as concomitant work opportunities that don't displace existing private or public sector workers.

A NATION OF LAWS

The only way that the land of opportunity works for everyone is if we truly act as the nation of laws that we fancy ourselves to be. We should not tolerate welfare benefits abuse, income tax fraud, or failure to pay child support anymore than we should tolerate assault, driving under the influence, or drug dealing - none of the myriad of crimes against our citizens, communities, and government. Not a day passes that we don't observe or read in the news about drivers running red lights or driving under the influence, robbers frightening shoppers with smash-and-grab thefts at retail stores, criminals stealing peoples' cars at gunpoint, welfare recipients repeatedly getting impregnated by different men and withholding information about the fathers in order to increase welfare benefits without financial responsibility, greedy millionaires underreporting their taxable income, celebrities cheating on their children's college admissions, illegal migrants ignoring asylum interview requirements, gangs importing drugs and causing the needless premature deaths of young people, online scammers taking advantage of seniors to gain access to their personal information and money, hackers invading the computer networks of organizations to hold their operations hostage to ransom demands, etc., etc., ad nauseam.

It is truly staggering when you think about all of the criminality that surrounds us. Not only is it frightening to some, it is discouraging to many who abide by our laws and play by the rules, yet see so many of their fellow residents getting away with flouting the rules and breaking the law. It is not fair to honorable citizens to allow such dishonorable behavior to go unregulated or unpunished. We are a nation of laws but are tolerating way too much lawlessness.

The genesis of this criminality finds its roots in a deficiency of respect for people, for property and for law enforcement. Absent a citizenry demonstrating mutual respect and self-restraint, we cannot hire an unlimited number of police officers, prosecutors, and judges, or build enough prisons to keep our communities safe and our nation functioning. And besides, who wants to live in a police state? But metastasizing criminality will diminish the health of this land of opportunity if it goes unchecked. So, how do we sustain America's promise as the land of liberty and of opportunity?

Respect begins with self-respect, which is first learned at home, in school, and through well supervised activities such as scouting and sports. Sadly, and for a variety of reasons, many of our fellow citizens did not benefit from such positive, formative experiences. But that does not exempt them from a society-wide obligation to comply with the laws that govern all of us. So those laws need to be taught in school, via public service messaging, in community education courses, and for criminals, in mandatory civic responsibility programs.

You can't hold someone to a standard of behavior if they don't know what that standard is. So, if respect for self and others does not organically generate positive behavior within the residents of a community, then positive behavior needs to be taught, encouraged, and reinforced throughout that community. After such orientation and awareness are accomplished, anyone's engagement in negative behavior needs to be addressed, admonished, and accounted for. Repeat offenders, who show a blatant disregard for the rights, property, and wellbeing of others, earn for themselves predictable punishment proportional to the gravity and consequences of their offenses. That is fair; it encourages others to not make the same mistakes, and it reassures law abiding residents that their communities are indeed sanctuaries of fairness and safety. In short, everyone needs to be afforded the important life lesson that positive benefits accrue to good behavior while negative results accrue to bad behavior.

JUDGING BEHAVIOR, NOT APPEARANCE

A discussion about the opportunities for a decent life afforded by America would not be complete without raising the topic of how we judge people - and we all do. Part of it is our survival instinct that has the primitive part of our brain always making quick judgments about possible dangers lurking - a dinosaur, a lion, a thief, a stalker, or a rapist. We can't help ourselves and should not feel guilty about this instinctual self-preservation.

We do, however, need to assess the basis upon which we judge people. It almost goes without saying, but sadly still needs to be said, that it should not be based upon appearance. The color of someone's skin, facial features, hair texture, whether they wear a hat or a turban, whether they speak English with or without an accent, etc., tells us nothing about whether they do or do not respect community standards of acceptable behavior and obey our laws.

What is telling, and what we necessarily should judge, is behavior. A person driving down the street with their windows open and car stereo blaring deserves to be judged as rude, simply because of their behavior. Imposing on others is

160

impolite, sometimes disturbing, and deserves to be called out, irrespective of their appearance. A Muslim woman wearing a burqa on a hot summer's day may stand out in our community, but it should only elicit our sympathy for her possible heat discomfort, not disrespectful commentary about her religious practices. Conversely, a woman wearing a cross around her neck while physically abusing her child in a store should elicit our concern enough to alert the store manager. Making judgments about others is a necessary element of self-preservation, especially when observed behavior is threatening. A drunk guy of any ethnicity or race passed out on a subway car is not a threat, but any guy ranting and brandishing a weapon on a subway car is a threat. It is behavior, not appearance, that is the only legitimate basis upon which to judge people fairly and react sensibly.

I learned a profoundly important lesson as a young man while serving in the military - which outpaced civilian society in confronting racism - that your race, ethnicity, geographical roots, dialect, religion, or other distinguishing characteristics were irrelevant to the mission. All that mattered was competence, mutual respect, and commitment to achieving a shared goal. Everyone understood that deviation from any of those would invite remedial action, loss of privileges, or dishonorable discharge. Severe deviations could be prosecutable under the Uniform Code of Military Justice. Needless to say, most military servicemen and women didn't deviate. Indeed, one could argue that their willingness to serve their country reflects an inherent respect that extends from themselves, to other people and to their country. Notwithstanding a few reported incidents of dishonorable behavior within the military, civilians could learn a lot from observing the behavior of the majority of our servicemen and women in how they treat one another with mutual respect and mutual care.

Fighting against our own often inherited prejudices can start immediately and simply by embracing the obvious truth that, irrespective of differences in our outward appearance, we are, basically, all pink on the inside. We all breathe, eat, and sleep; we experience emotions ranging from hope and anticipation to insecurity and fear; we can all get fatigued, lonely, and depressed at times and can also experience happiness, inspiration, and joy. The blood coursing through all of our bodies bleeds red no matter the color of our skin. We are all humans deserving of respect no matter our differences, and we are all accountable to the same Creator.

Respecting people sounds simple enough, but it can be a challenge to overcome our tribal mindset that sees others as different and potentially threatening. Two stories illustrate how ingrained our prejudices can be. I had been invited to go to Harlem to meet a formerly homeless man whom I had mentored years earlier through an education outreach program of Catholic Charities. Our life experiences and appearances could not have been more different. As a white guy in a business suit, I was admittedly a bit apprehensive walking through a largely African American neighborhood which had had a reputation of being a bit dangerous. Needless to say, when I finally found my friend on the street, I was relieved. I also marveled at how he was known to so many folks walking by who called out his name and high fived him. As a white guy, I felt less vulnerable by having my African American friend walking with me through a black neighborhood where whites were an obvious minority.

These prejudices and fears are a two way street. My wife and I had invited a former corporate banking colleague and African American friend to visit us at our home. To my surprise, he was reluctant to come because it was a largely white neighborhood. I assuaged his concerns by meeting him at the subway station and walking with him to our co-op building. Not surprisingly, we had a very interesting conversation about how we can perceive and fear others simply because their appearance is different than our own.

By the way, years earlier, this former banking colleague of mine in Manhattan who had transferred to the bank's Los Angeles office told me a story that was both eye-opening and upsetting. One weekend, shortly after moving there, while he was still driving a rented car, he drove into his apartment complex parking lot and was followed there and confronted by police officers. After he produced relevant documents to prove his identity, address and eligibility to drive the vehicle, he asked the police officers why they pulled him over. Their response was, "You didn't look like you belonged here." This is an Ivy League college graduate, working for one of the largest banks in the country, whose business attire during the week is as preppy as it gets. Unfortunately and unfairly for him, he was wearing casual clothes on that Saturday, presenting a prejudicially less respect-worthy appearance, something that I, as a white person, wouldn't need to think twice about. White privilege, of which we may not be consciously aware, nonetheless does exist.

In fairness to the police, had his driving been erratic, if the license plate was missing from the vehicle, if he failed to signal his turns, any of those would have been a defensible basis for the police to pull him over because those are behaviors that contravene community standards and state laws. But to pull him over just for his appearance was insulting to him. Hearing about it angered me because you could not find a more standup guy than my friend. It was an important learning experience for me as a white guy as to how black guys are prejudicially judged. My friend took it in stride because it was not the first time he said his being black garnered inappropriate attention and inquiry. We all deserve - and we all can do - better than this.

The government can change laws, but it cannot change hearts. The best way to challenge our own unconscious

163

prejudices is to get to know those who are different than us - in appearance, employment, religion, food preferences, choice of music, gender identification, ethnic background, political posture, etc. Each of us prefers to be known for who we are as an individual, not as part of a demographic category. Instead of making assumptions about those who differ from us, get to know them on a person-to-person level and you will likely find that they are not so different than you. Indeed, you may find that you have a lot more in common than you realize - in sense of humor, love of animals, military or other public service, favorite vacation venues, driving experiences, complaints about crime, commuting nightmares, aspirations for themselves and loved ones, concern about affording retirement, caring for an elderly relative, etc.

This is not to diminish the differences that we may have in a wide variety of things - musical tastes, preferred dog breeds, favorite television channels, frequented stores, religious beliefs, public policy positions, political candidates, etc. Think of a Venn Diagram which uses overlapping circles to illustrate similarities and differences. If we are going to achieve our potential as a 'more perfect union' and thrive in this land of opportunity, we need to mostly live within the overlapping circles - embracing the commonalities that we share with our fellow citizens. We may not like some of the things about which we may differ with other people, and that's okay. They are making choices as to how they wish to live, whom they wish to love, who they want to hold public office, etc. We can disagree with their choices, but we need to respect them as people, even when we may hold diametrically opposing views on a particular subject. We can and should engage in respectful conversations about differences so that we can try to understand why someone feels the way that they do and what their unique life experiences have instilled in them, and reciprocate by sharing how our particular life experiences have influenced our choices and shaped our opinions.

At the end of the day, after we have given voice to our opinions and listened to others', expressed our feelings and empathized with theirs,' and taken action aligned with our values just as they do with theirs,' we need to step back into those overlapping circles where we find agreement on the matters universally acknowledged as essential to dignity and prosperity while cohabitating in our land of opportunity.

SHARED MORAL VALUES

There is no such thing as a nation with no values. Nations do not exist in a values vacuum. It is inherent in human experience that values always exist. They may not be conscious, they may be imposed, they may be as simple as self-indulgence above all else and they may change over time, but exist they do.

We don't live in a theoretical construct, but in a real flesh-and-blood world. For example, in our lifetime, we saw in Soviet Communism the denial of God and the glorification of the state. The theory of communism, derived primarily from Karl Marx, advocated for a classless society in which all property is publicly owned, everyone works, and each is paid according to their abilities and needs. Communism in practice in the Soviet Union made the state its god, enabling the state to do whatever it considered necessary for the state to continue - crush public protest, lock up dissidents, murder opposition candidates, and even fatally shoot people trying to escape the communist state's borders.

This last point was made poignantly clear to me as a teenager when watching an evening news broadcast about some people trying to flee Communist East Berlin to get to Democratic West Berlin - geographically the same city but separated by a wall guarded by armed soldiers. Seeing several poor souls gunned down as they tried to scale the wall and run away prompted two thoughts in my adolescent mind, *'How bad can life be behind the Iron Curtain that people risk almost certain death trying to escape?'* and *'Why won't their government just let them travel if they want to leave?'*

165

I was fortunate to be able to learn early in life about the plague that is Communism from my father, who had worked for the U.S. State Department and been posted to our embassy in Bucharest, Romania, after World War II. His stories of what he saw Romanians experience under their Communist rulers were shocking to my young, naïve sense of the freedom and abundance that we experience in America. It was a lesson that stayed with me years later when I served in the U.S. Air Force under top secret clearance monitoring Soviet military activities in the Black Sea area. We were in a Cold War, the freedom-loving West against the oppressive Communist Soviet Union comprised of 15 republics straddling much of northern Eurasia from the Baltic and Black Seas to the Pacific Ocean, both us and them armed with enough nuclear weapons to destroy the entire planet many times over.

But the Cold War was not that of two armies envying each other's territories, natural resources, access to warm water ports, etc. It was a standoff of diametrically opposite values - the West's embrace of individual liberty, economic freedom, and self-government as opposed to the Soviet Union's subjugating the individual person, outlawing individual initiative and demanding adherence to the dictatorial governance of a communist regime, which suppresses speech, censors information and even encourages spying on each other's neighbors. Communism brooks no challenges to the demands of the almighty state, however dignity denying or murderous the state's actions may be.

Values exist everywhere on a continuum from benign to malignant, and they have a profound impact upon the quality of humans' real world lives. In 1983, at the height of the Cold War, then-U.S. President Ronald Reagan gave an historic speech in which he referred to the Soviet Union as an *"evil empire"* and *"the focus of evil in the modern world."* Although the Soviet Union collapsed in 1991, which ushered in great Western optimism that Russia and its former satellite states might embrace individual liberty and democracy, we have more recently learned that the evil empire simply had a setback from its nearly seven decade rule from 1922 to 1991.

It's worth noting that during the period 1985 to 1990, current Russian President Vladimir Putin had worked in Dresden, East Germany as a KGB liaison officer to the Stasi secret police. After moving up the ranks of the Soviet Government, starting in 1999, he held positions as Prime Minister or President to the present day, the longest serving Russian leader since the murderous reign of Joseph Stalin. Infamously, in 2005, during an address to Russia's political elites, Putin said that the collapse of the Soviet empire *"was the greatest geopolitical catastrophe of the century."*

In 2014, with Putin's first incursion into eastern Ukraine, and more dramatically with his 2022 invasion of Ukraine, we have seen the same evil reemerge in unprovoked attacks on innocent civilians and communities' infrastructure, sparing neither children, women nor the elderly in bombing schools, hospitals, theaters, apartment buildings and trying to obliterate the distinctive identity of an entire people - denying life, the antithesis of affirming life. Just like those who lived before us, in our lifetimes, we are witnessing evil personified again, perpetuated by another generation of fellow humans, each a moral agent choosing to embrace evil values rather than noble values.

So, when considering shared values that sustain our land of opportunity, we first must acknowledge that deciding which values to embrace is a moral choice. We may have inherited certain values from our elders, we may be influenced by what we observe in the media, and we may be prejudiced in our retention of some, and rejection of other values, but they cannot be denied. We all, consciously or unconsciously, live by certain values. There is no such thing as creating a value free, morally neutral land in which to live. As free moral agents, we choose the values by which we live.

I would posit that the most life-affirming and dignity-enhancing values for a land of genuine opportunity find their origin in the Judeo Christian teachings, starting with the Ten Commandments. Although they are 'religious' by definition, they are 'universal' in their respect for human dignity irrespective of religious orientation or lack thereof.

Few people are totally unfamiliar with these commandments. Indeed, if you put all ten of the commandments into contemporary parlance, it becomes clear that we humans would go a long way toward relieving moral ambiguity, resolving culture wars, and limiting our moral failures and consequent life-disruptions, if we incorporated these commandments into our lives. It's worth noting that these words, believed by many to come from God, are not presented as suggestions, recommendations, or requests. They are commandments, as in, fail to do them at your own peril. We need to look no further than the aforementioned example of the Soviet Union as a warning of how evil thrives when God is denied.

So, with obvious literary liberties, I share as a modern twist 'God's Timeless Top Ten List' for us free-willed moral agents. As you read through them, think about how embracing them would enhance our present culture, heal divisiveness, and build a more solid foundation for us to thrive in our land of opportunity.

ONE, honor God who created you. Be humble enough to admit that you didn't create yourself, that one can neither prove nor disprove God's existence, and that, since God reportedly wrote the owner's manual for you, you'd be well advised to read His FAQs.

TWO, don't create or worship false Gods. That doesn't just mean other deities; it includes money, sex, power, celebrity, ideology, drugs, or any person or thing that you might put above your loyalty to God.

168

THREE, don't use God's name in vain. Be creative. There are virtually an unlimited number of other words that you can use to express yourself. Leave that one alone.

FOUR, don't work every day. Take at least one day off for yourself and your family that God gave to us. Trust Him. You'll be happier, your health will be better, and your social life will be more satisfying.

FIVE, honor your parents. They're not perfect, but they did the best they could, under circumstances you may not be privy to. If you forgive them their faults, while protecting yourself from any possible emotional or physical abuse, you will have more peace when they pass away. And if you can give them some joy in their old age, perhaps someone will do the same for you.

SIX, don't kill anyone or anything. Every creature, human and animal, loves its life and deserves to be able to live its entire natural course. If you must kill, only do so in defense of self or others, or for safety or survival.

SEVEN, don't commit adultery. It is deeply damaging to the self, to others, and to relationships. There are pros and cons of single life and of married life. Think before you choose one or the other. If you want the joys and benefits of married life, you must accept its limitations and responsibilities.

EIGHT, don't steal. That includes not just tangible things like money and possessions, but also intangible things like stealing someone's place ahead of you in a line or on a highway entrance ramp, stealing others' ideas in writing, music, imagery, or any type of intellectual property, stealing people's freedom to choose their preferred reading, their bodily autonomy, their joy of loving whomever they wish, etc. Just don't take what doesn't belong to you.

NINE, don't lie. That includes not withholding accurate information, not misrepresenting, not falsely accusing, not repeating gossip, rumors, or conspiracies, not creating

169

misleading images or videos, etc. Speak and spread only the truth, and let your "yes" be yes and your "no" be no.

TEN, don't be jealous of others. Don't allow yourself to fall victim to media advertising and images which exploit that vulnerability. There will always be those who have more and those who have less. Develop an attitude of gratitude for what you have, be generous with your time, talent, and treasure, and be forgiving toward those who may wish you ill.

It is hard to imagine that, as a nation, we would be worse off; indeed, it is far more likely that we would be better off in our land of opportunity, that is, America, if we respect God's insights into our humanity, no matter how complex our society, sophisticated our technology or challenging are the changes to which we need to adapt. His values become especially critical in our modern world of relativism, where falsehoods are turbocharged as technology accelerates and challenges abound, which is becoming exponentially more consequential to self-worth, human dignity, and the shared cultural values which are core to our land of opportunity.

What We Can Do

It is incumbent upon all citizens to become informed about the critical issues facing our nation and our communities. With our rights come responsibilities, not the least of which is making informed choices at the ballot box. To help in this regard, below is a Candidate Evaluation checklist which you can use to evaluate politicians campaigning for your vote to hold public office. Assess them yourself and decide which candidate is best prepared and most likely to take a transpartisan common sense approach toward strengthening our shared land of opportunity by advancing personal and civic responsibility.

170

Candidate Evaluation Criteria

	Candidate _____'s Position on Opportunity and Responsibility	Yes/No
1	Supports educational campaigns that encourage work and self-reliance	
2	Advances efforts to improve the eligibility and effectiveness of public welfare programs	
3	Tightens enforcement of child support from baby fathers	
4	Works to increase affordability and access to child care	
5	Advocates for education and vocational training to secure better paying jobs	
6	Equips government agencies to prosecute individual and organizational fraud	
7	Supports expanding the teaching of civic responsibilities and laws throughout society	
8	Encourages judging people on behavior and admonishes judging people on appearance	
9	Provides for the teaching of good moral values in our schools, media, and institutions	
10	Sets an example as a public official of making morally sound choices	

The information, data and statistics mentioned came from a wide variety of open sources available over the internet. A debt of gratitude is expressed for the hard work of all those people at so many different private and public sector organizations who spend countless hours collecting and collating data, researching information, verifying facts, and producing reports for public consumption, which profoundly facilitates the creation of an informed citizenry upon which our democracy depends. Among those sources:

Migration Policy Institute

Statista.com

World.Population.Review.com

Wikipedia

"Public and Private Families," Andrew Cherlin (2009)

"Success Stories," Joe Soss (2002)

Center on Budget and Policy Priorities

National Women's Law Center

The New Republic, September 2006

Google

Economist.com

USDA.gov

USAFacts.org

Ensuring Political Integrity

Balancing Citizen and Corporate Interests

Our forefathers were wise in crafting the structure of our government as a triangular relationship among the legislative, executive, and judicial branches. They knew how easily power could be consolidated and exercised for the narrow interests of the few over the many. What they could not have envisioned was the emergence of a shadow influence on our government that is neither elected by voters, nor appointed by public officials, yet wields tremendous influence in the halls of government - lobbyists. There are tens of thousands of lobbyists in Washington, DC, as well as in our state capitols, pushing their clients' agendas that are not always in the public's best interest.

For a jaw-dropping look at how much money is being spent annually on lobbying, you may wish to peruse the web site of OpenSecrets.org, which is a nonpartisan, independent, and nonprofit research group that tracks money in U.S. politics and its effects on elections and public policy.

As they note, the 2010 Citizens United vs. Federal Election Commission Supreme Court decision permitted corporations and unions to make political expenditures from their treasuries directly and through other organizations, as long as the spending, often in the form of television advertisements, is done independently of a particular candidate. Often, there is incomplete disclosure about who is funding it, which precludes voters from knowing who is actually behind many political advertisements.

According to U.S. News and World Report, the U.S. Chamber of Commerce, which mostly represents the interests of large industries, like tobacco, banking, and fossil fuels, seeks favorable treatment for them through trade negotiations, tax treatment, regulations, and judicial rulings. As the Chamber's website notes among its membership benefits, *"Joining the U.S. Chamber of Commerce will provide you with instant access to one of the largest business networks available. We are the strongest, most active business advocacy group in the country, with a professional staff of hundreds of the nation's top policy experts, lobbyists, lawyers, and communicators."* So, for example, it should come as no surprise that it has resisted the science on climate change and fought policy action to lower carbon emissions.

Another example is the Pharmaceutical Research and Manufacturers of America, that spends hundreds of millions of dollars trying to influence politicians, which may help explain why our prescription drug costs are so much higher than in other countries. The tech industry spends huge sums to limit efforts to regulate technology companies which have come to have an outsize, and sometimes harmful, influence in our society - which compels urgent attention.

The U.S. Surgeon General recently warned of dangers to our youngsters, citing a 2019 study published in the Journal of the American Medical Association, that showed that teenagers who spend three hours per day on social media double their risk of depression. This is consistent with periodic media reports of children who killed themselves because of online bullying. And think about the adult victims of online scammers who have bilked Americans from billions of dollars. The FBI estimates that these so-called 'pig butchering' scams stole almost $4 billion from tens of thousands of victims last year, and it's increasing annually. The profit driven algorithms of many online sites has created a wild west dynamic on the internet, which begs for sensible regulations which are too often resisted by many tech companies and their lobbyists.

While there is nothing illegal or morally wrong with organizations communicating their take on issues to our government, the influence of special interests is grossly out of balance with advocacy for the interests of average Americans.

The money-fueled relationships between lobbyists and legislators help to explain why seemingly solvable American problems persist unresolved. For example, given the power and influence of the National Rifle Association (NRA), is it just a coincidence that effective gun control efforts flounder while mass shootings occur with such frequency and gut-wrenching carnage?

Labor unions representing workers have much smaller lobbying power compared to that of big business. Decades of economic data demonstrate that labor unions improve the well-being of the middle class by raising incomes, increasing workplace safety, and improving work environments and job satisfaction. Unfortunately, union membership peaked in the 1950s at one-third of the U.S. workforce, and is now down to just ten-percent. Is it any wonder why, over this period, middle-class American households have experienced stagnating wages, rising income volatility, and reduced intergenerational mobility - even as big corporations have prospered with record profits and huge compensation packages for their executives? Part of the decline in union membership can be ascribed to the transformation of our country from an industrial to an increasingly service driven economy, and to the off-shoring of many manufacturing jobs to other countries. But service workers are no less in need of representation, an argument lost on many companies which are fighting union organizing efforts.

Unions play a critical role in our society by accomplishing for workers what workers cannot accomplish on their own. Historically, unions have substantially improved the quality of American life by shortening the work week in 1870 from 61 hours to 40 hours, ending child labor in 1938, and advancing workers compensation laws, paid family leave, unemployment benefits, and employer-based health insurance coverage. Today, unions continue to champion equal rights and equal pay, fight discrimination against race, gender, sexual

175

orientation, and disability, and promote flexible work schedules, maternity rights, and paternity pay so that child care responsibilities can be shared in American families. In short, unions foster respect and dignity in the workplace, so their declining influence in the economy and diminished voice in our public discourse is a matter of great concern if we expect our elected representatives to develop a fair, balanced, and comprehensive understanding of the issues on which they legislate. The reality is that it is difficult for politicians to legislate fairly in the interests of American workers when some legislators are taking money from anti-union organizations.

Exacerbating the outsize influence of corporate over citizen interests is that several hundred former members of Congress and agency heads are active lobbyists, and hundreds of lobbyists previously worked in senior government positions. With clever political strategies, deep financial pockets, and, for some, connections established while in public service, lobbyists present to our elected representatives and agency directors carefully prepared positions that help launch or derail legislation, change laws, and write regulations – sometimes with a negative tangible impact on the health, safety, livelihoods, and quality of life of Americans.

What does the business community - that inherently seeks to profit from its expenditures – expect to gain from its influence peddling? Here are just three examples.

LIMITING MINIMUM WAGE INCREASES

Many business associations argue against minimum wage increases as dangerously inflationary and that they reduce employment opportunities for the least skilled. Yet studies conducted by the Economic Policy Institute on minimum wage increases failed to find systematic, significant job loss associated with wage increases. More precise economic models that analyze low-wage markets, in particular, indicate that employers are often able to absorb some of the costs of a wage increase through higher productivity, decreased absenteeism, and increased worker morale. Even a study of state minimum wages by the Fiscal Policy Institute found no evidence of negative employment effects on small businesses. Yet business lobbyists fight against increases in the federal minimum wage. One might ask, how many business executives and their lobbyists are willing to forego pay raises and bonuses for themselves? Do they consider their salary increases dangerously inflationary?

Seen in the context of welfare reform that has compelled more poor families to move from welfare to workfare, which makes them more reliant upon income from low-paying jobs, minimum wage increases tend to have a positive effect on reducing poverty. Since the 1970s, the gap between rich and poor in the United States has widened. Of course, we can't blame this just on long-delayed increases in the minimum wage. But we do know that free markets, technology, and globalization tend to erode wages at the bottom, while tending to increase compensation at the top. Yet, during years of rapid technological change and unfettered global markets, we have not done enough to adjust wages for low-income workers. Many economists and sociologists report that in recent decades, the typical child starting out in poverty in the United States would have a better chance at prosperity if they grew up in Europe or Canada.

The idea of paying American employees a living wage is seemingly lost on many within our business community, as well as upon those elected officials who advance business interests above the interests of their constituents. Common sense tells us that this is not an equitable governmental balancing of citizen and corporate interests.

MAKING PERSONAL BANKRUPTCY MORE DIFFICULT

Tens of thousands of Americans, including the unemployed, sick, and divorced, have had to file for Chapter 7 bankruptcy. The banking lobby succeeded in convincing our federal government to change the personal bankruptcy law to make it more difficult for Americans to qualify for Chapter 7 protections, which can erase all debts and give people a chance to get back on their feet financially. Although consumers are responsible for managing their own financial obligations, many people resort to bankruptcy not because of profligate spending, but because of overwhelming medical expenses, exhausted unemployment benefits, market losses in their retirement accounts, unexpectedly reduced pensions, loss of income due to disability, or the accumulated costs of single parenting after divorce. Why did the banking industry push for the change?

The credit card companies deliberately moved into the 'sub-prime market' – their euphemism for borrowers with checkered credit histories – for which they charge a higher interest rate for greater default risk. They offer easy credit on such attractive terms that many people can't resist. Some get 'hooked' on buying on credit. Even though a small percentage of customers default, the card issuers already accommodate for this in establishing their higher interest rates and loan loss reserves.

Although this enabled the credit card companies to earn tremendous profits, that apparently wasn't enough. The card companies wanted consumers, many of whom are already on the brink of financial collapse, to reduce the industry's loan loss rate further and increase their profits that much more - at the cost of making it even harder for families overwhelmed with debt to have a second chance at getting their financial house in order.

It seems a bit disingenuous that the credit card companies inundate Americans with credit offers that result in some people getting in over their heads, but when debt-saddled consumers hit bottom and finally want to break themselves of the credit habit, the card companies can now make their chance at rehabilitation through bankruptcy less accessible. Is it any wonder that banks and credit card companies are among the biggest contributors to politicians?

LIMITING FINANCIAL INDUSTRY REGULATION

Among capitalist economies with public markets for trading stocks and bonds, America is unequalled for developing a financial market in which increasing numbers of citizens can participate. Yet as financial scandals have brought to our attention, perhaps our confidence should be tempered. Why? Due to the lobbying of investment and brokerage houses, the American financial market has been kept largely self-regulated. Although our tax dollars pay for the Securities and Exchange Commission (SEC) as a line of defense against illegal securities trading and fraudulent financial reporting, the reality is that the SEC has for years been grossly underfunded and inadequately staffed to be able to effectively monitor the thousands of investment banks, brokers and dealers with whom millions of Americans entrust their hard earned money. While most financial houses and corporations conduct business legally and ethically, not all do so consistently. Common sense would tell any reasonable person that relying upon the 'wolf to guard the hen house' - no matter how much of a straight shooter the wolf appears to be - is unwise. But the industry lobbied hard for self-regulation and won. Some Americans' 401K retirement plans and investment portfolios haven't been so lucky.

It should come as no surprise that our sophisticated financial industry has one of the most powerful lobbying efforts in Washington - an assemblage of intellectual, financial, and relationship capital readily available to derail the occasional legislative attempt to adopt regulations that would provide more effective oversight of the industry. Thanks especially to the initiatives of some courageous State Attorneys General, more companies are now being carefully scrutinized and, in some cases, having to pay large settlements and change business practices. But it's a bit late when you consider that comprehensive regulatory oversight might have precluded the scandals and losses in the first place. American citizens who lost money due to 'financial irregularities' – i.e., fraud - should look to their Senators and Congressmen for an explanation of how they allowed this interest group to influence them to the point where the oversight presumably afforded by the SEC was completely overwhelmed by interest group arguments that the securities industry could police itself.

So ubiquitous are lobbyists that even foreign organizations hire them in the United States. One issue of particular concern, is dissuading our U.S. Congress from passing laws that would limit outsourcing of American jobs by American companies so that these other countries' residents can perform the jobs that American workers used to perform. To counter balance the inherent corporate drive to generate profits wherever and however they can, there need to be guardrails on those activities to ensure that American workers are prioritized with opportunities to develop and utilize their skills to make a living in our country over enabling foreign workers to take jobs that Americans are capable of performing. If the pandemic taught us anything, it's that we should not depend upon foreign workers and suppliers for our goods, particularly in critical areas like healthcare, computer parts, and the military.

Other than some limited registration and disclosure requirements, lobbyists are essentially unregulated. Their activities largely go unreported since most of their work is done behind closed doors. And most trade associations that hire many of them are not required to disclose their donors. These associations and their hired gun lobbyists have grown so powerful that they are a force to be reckoned with by virtually every candidate and elected official. Candidates cannot hope to gain office, let alone hold it beyond a single term, without granting moneyed lobbyists access to advocate on behalf of a company, industry, trade group, or foreign country.

Officially, of course, no votes are bought. But don't think for a minute that their requests go unheard. They get heard loud and clear. In fact, lobbyists often submit to our public officials their preferred language for specific legislation and regulations. Who, you might rhetorically ask, has equal access, power, and influence to advocate on behalf of average American citizens?

A growing trend in influencing government is corporate funded trips - carrying our public officials, and sometimes their spouses, to attend industry conferences, tour manufacturing plants, speak at meetings, or enjoy a vacation. Since the trips are paid by corporations and trade associations they are allowed under Congressional rules. Why? Because only travel paid by registered lobbyists and foreign agents is prohibited. Although our lawmakers are limited to accepting meals, gifts or expenses, most Congressional ethics rules don't apply to trips considered 'educational.'

Public interest groups sensibly argue that if corporate trips are genuinely educational, they should be paid by the government and not by special interests. Their argument is compelling if we don't want to taint the objectivity and impartiality of our public officials in exercising their authority.

Perhaps of even greater concern is that the United State Supreme Court doesn't have any enforceable ethical behavior rules at all. Think about that: no ethical behavior rules for the life tenured justices of our country's highest court, which issues rulings that have a profound influence and lasting impact on life in America.

Each American has the right to petition our elected representatives. Lobbyists argue they are simply providing our legislators and regulators with information. What's different between the petition of an individual citizen and that of a professional lobbyist is money, power, and connections. Who does your common sense tell you will get the Senator, Congressman, or Agency Head's attention, influence, and perhaps even favorable decision? Politicians, like the rest of us, prefer to win. But politicians are now so structurally dependent within our electoral system upon the money of special interests to fund their campaigns that they tend to be far more attentive to their requests than to what's best for their constituents or for the country overall.

To attempt to redress the heavy conservative influence of business, liberal-leaning lobby groups emerged, resulting in a competitive and costly free-for-all among different groups lobbying for special attention for each of their issues of concern. The forest products industry lobbies to open up timberland, while the environmentalists lobby to protect wilderness areas. The medical associations lobby to put a cap on malpractice judgments, while the trial lawyers lobby to leave settlements uncapped. And on and on and on. What is being squandered is broad citizen representation, in favor of narrow group representation, while what's best for the country as a larger community of citizens is lost in the shuffle of professional advocacy, political contributions, and personal perquisites.

So, how do we get out of this predicament where citizen interests are being sacrificed to special interest groups and bring more integrity into our political system? Four suggestions:

FIRST, cap campaign spending and campaign durations. Other democracies do it, and their candidates are no less able to get their messages out to voters. Look at Britain, our closest ally and just as much a political democracy and capitalist economy as the United States. Their formula limits each candidate's expenditure per district plus a certain amount per eligible voter and limits the period of campaigning. The parties can spend a further amount for each contested seat within a national maximum. On a comparative per capita basis, the major British parties and their candidates spend a fraction per eligible voter as compared to our Republican and Democratic parties in the United States. Imagine if our elected officials spent less money and less time fundraising and campaigning and more attention and time actually governing. Just imagine.

182

SECOND, redirect the transfer of monies to fund campaigns for public office. If there would be no monies received directly by a politician from special interests, then presumably there would be no leverage to expect special interest favors from that politician. This idea isn't alien to Congress, that already created a public funding program using the optional check-off on our income tax returns to reduce the role of large private political contributions. But it's limited to presidential elections only and is woefully underfunded.

So, instead of individuals and organizations contributing directly to politicians, their campaigns, and their political parties, we could have individuals and organizations contribute to a public fund from which monies are disbursed equitably to the political parties to fund their politicians' campaigns. If voters push Congress to take this initiative further by having campaigns for all elective offices financed only with public money, then American elections would better represent our democracy's founding principle of government of the people, by the people, and for the people, and politicians' attention would naturally shift to the citizenry as a whole and away from lobbyists pushing their organizations' narrow agendas.

THIRD, make illegal the acceptance of money, largesse, and perquisites from any source by all government officials. Their taxpayer-paid salaries, staff, offices and travel reimbursements should be adequate to conduct the people's business. Instead of the current practice of playing around the edges with different iterations of campaign finance reform, parsing words in rules of ethics governing different office holders, and disingenuously defining the purposes of travel, completely remove all special interest money from the halls of power in Washington and each state capitol. The perception of influence, let alone its substance, has a corrupting effect on the electoral and governance processes and undermines voter confidence. Without special interest contributions, businesses and other groups would still be able to communicate their positions and problems through their submission of position papers, studies, surveys, correspondence, etc. But their arguments would have to be persuasive on the merits, not on the influence to give or withhold money for the legislator's reelection or the agency director's entertainment.

FOURTH, reform the rules governing justices of our United States Supreme Court. For example, the United States is the only major constitutional democracy that gives lifetime appointments to its high court justices. Since the lifetime justices of the Supreme Court of the United States (SCOTUS) are appointed by the then sitting president, the timing of appointments is arbitrary, based solely upon when a sitting judge may decide to retire, or dies, creating a vacancy. This unpredictable timing of lifetime appointments can result in justices sitting for multiple decades, rendering profoundly influential judicial decisions that impact Americans for generations. We know that it has resulted in multiple judges being appointed by a single president while some presidents were unable to appoint even a single judge.

We don't want judges to have term durations that are too short lest they be subject to undue political influence. But we also don't want a single president being able to 'stack the court' with multiple appointees whose judicial philosophy aligns with that particular president.

Our other two branches of national government are subject to in office limits - presidents to four years, senators to six years, and congressmen to two years. Perhaps we should limit the terms of SCOTUS justices to twelve years, the equivalent of three four-year presidential terms, to ensure that the court's makeup changes with some degree of regularity and to limit the chance that any single president can appoint several justices whose influence can last for generations, as happened recently with a former president appointing three judges during his one presidential term.

Another example of needed reform would be to hold SCOTUS justices to the same ethics rules that apply to the holders of office in our executive and legislative branches of government, including restrictions on receiving, and disclosure requirements for, financial or in-kind gifts of any type. Justices should also be required to recuse themselves from any cases in which they or any family members have a financial or other conflict of interest.

And, in light of the recent shocking SCOTUS ruling that grants presidents immunity for criminal actions committed as part of their 'official duties,' we need a constitutional amendment that aligns with our founding fathers' beliefs that a president's power is not absolute - as in a monarchy which they knew all too well - and that no one is above the law, which has been an article of faith among all Americans for generations. What we never had to imagine before this ill-advised ruling of our country's highest court we now have to imagine: any president would be able to ascribe any action they take as falling under their official duties. Considering how much power we entrust with the President of the United States (POTUS), as chief executive of the country, chief diplomat, and commander-in-chief of our armed forces, the idea of them being given carte blanche to take even criminal action with impunity defies common sense, historical constitutional interpretation and our country's traditions.

A carefully crafted constitutional amendment - which would require a two-thirds vote of both Houses of Congress, or would have to be requested and ratified by three-fourths of our State Legislatures - would not limit the powers of the presidency, but would simply clarify that the Constitution does not confer any immunity from federal criminal indictment, trial, conviction or sentencing by virtue of having served as president.

These four suggestions would help imbue our electoral, governance, and judicial processes with greater integrity in the eyes of voters, would liberate our politicians from excessive focus on narrow corporate interests in favor of paying greater attention to broader citizen interests, and might tip the scales toward more citizen confidence in our three independent branches of government. This may yield greater voter turnout at elections which is essential to a vibrant democracy.

No doubt those currently feeding at the trough of current campaign practices would be up in arms if these suggestions were adopted. First to complain would be the lobbyists who, legally precluded from using their sponsoring corporations' money, would have to persuade legislators based on the inherent strength or weakness of their policy position. Second to balk would be the advertising agencies, television and radio stations, and other campaign vendors disgruntled about political candidates having less money to spend and less time to spend it. Third, to resist would be the political consultants whose jobs would be shortened in duration as campaigns would have to be run on less money in a shorter time frame. Sympathetic though we may be to the adjustments they would have to make, the country overall would benefit enormously. American citizens would be the winners of a reinvigorated electoral process devoid of the influence of special interest group money. Legislators, no longer beholden to the narrow interests of lobbyists, would be free to vote their conscience and genuinely represent all of their constituents. And all Americans could have greater confidence in the objectivity and integrity of our highest court's justices and the decisions that they render.

America has grown to be a large and diverse nation with a more sophisticated sense of fair play among our citizenry. Until we disempower the shadow influence of lobbyists on government, voters will remain suspicious of the integrity of our politicians, legislation and regulations will continue to largely serve special interests rather than all Americans, and our politicians will continue to be indebted to their financial benefactors. Our forefathers intended our democracy to deliver genuine citizen representation. Our country needs it, and our citizens deserve it. It's time for voters to reclaim their representation by demanding of government officials that special interest money no longer have a place in American elections, governance and jurisprudence.

What We Can Do

It is incumbent upon all citizens to become informed about the critical issues facing our nation and our communities. With our rights come responsibilities, not the least of which is making informed choices at the ballot box. To help in this regard, below is a Candidate Evaluation Criteria checklist which you can use to evaluate one politician as compared to another politician campaigning for your vote to hold public office. Assess them yourself and decide which candidate is best prepared and most likely to take a transpartisan common sense approach to campaign reform, conflicts of interest and ethics standards and keeping no one above the law.

Candidate Evaluation Criteria

	Candidate _____'s Position on Campaign Reform, Ethics, and Universally Applicable Law	Yes/No
1	Supports a cap on campaign spending based upon district or state demographics to not advantage one candidate over another	
2	Supports a short duration time frame before elections for politicians, political parties, and advocacy groups to campaign and advertise in any medium to reduce the amount of money campaigns need to raise, to have elected officials spend more time governing, and to better focus voters' attention closer to elections	
3	Advocates for closing loopholes on elected officials and appointed officials' acceptance of money, largesse, perquisites, jobs, contracts, etc., from private citizens and organizations before, during, and up to ten years after finishing public service	
4	Advocates for campaign finance reform that transforms organizations and individuals contributing directly to politicians, their campaigns, and their political parties in favor of contributing to a public fund from which monies are disbursed equitably to the political parties for their politicians	

5	Supports full public disclosure, no later than thirty days before an election, of all sources of financial or in-kind contributions to any candidate or campaign, the failure of which would disqualify the candidate's appearance on a ballot	
6	Favors strengthening ethics rules and enforcement for all executive, legislative, and judicial branch officials	
7	Advocates for the adoption of recusal requirements and term limits for justices of the U.S. Supreme Court	
8	Supports a constitutional amendment clarifying that presidents don't have immunity from federal criminal indictment, trial, conviction, or sentencing by virtue of having served as president	

The information, data and statistics mentioned came from a wide variety of open sources available over the internet. A debt of gratitude is expressed for the hard work of all those people at so many different private and public sector organizations who spend countless hours collecting and collating data, researching information, verifying facts, and producing reports for public consumption, which profoundly facilitates the creation of an informed citizenry upon which our democracy depends. Among those sources:

OpenSecrets.org

U.S. News and World Report

U.S. Department of the Treasury

Economic Policy Institute

Federal Bureau of Investigation

Fiscal Policy Institute

JAMA

Wikipedia

The New York Times

The Wall Street Journal

CivicsRenewalNetwork.org

GoodReads.com

Letters from an American, Heather Cox Richardson

Conclusion

Citizen Inspiration: Continuing the Legacy

We know from psychology that one must engage the head as well as the heart to achieve sustainable behavior change. The earlier chapters of this book were intended to appeal to our heads with a transpartisan common sense look at several critical issues facing our nation. One or more of these issues may resonate with you personally. Adopt them as your own and advocate for what you believe. This is, after all, our democracy to shape for the common good.

I conclude with some quotes intended to appeal to our hearts, words of wisdom from fellow Americans which can serve to inspire us to do the hard work of more thoughtfully and carefully vetting our politicians whom we should expect will bring to public office: common sense, compassion, competence, courage and civility in service of the common good. If we put our heads and our hearts into it, we can together strengthen our American democracy.

"Wherefore, instead of gazing at each other with suspicious or doubtful curiosity, let each of us hold out to his neighbor the hearty hand of friendship, and unite in drawing a line, which, like an act of oblivion, shall bury in forgetfulness every former dissention. Let the names of Whig and Tory be extinct; and let none other be heard among us, than those of good citizen; an open and resolute friend; and a virtuous supporter of the rights of mankind, and of the Free and Independent States Of America."

- Thomas Paine, American Founding Father and Author of "Common Sense" 1776

"The way to secure liberty is to place it in the people's hands, that is, to give them the power at all times to defend it in the legislature and in the courts of justice."

- President John Adams

"America is another name for opportunity."

- Ralph Waldo Emerson, Poet, Philosopher and Essayist

"We're blessed with the opportunity to stand for something - for liberty and freedom and fairness. And these things are worth fighting for, worth devoting our lives to."

- President Ronald Reagan

"No man is entitled to the blessings of freedom unless he be vigilant in its preservation."

- General Douglas MacArthur

"True patriotism springs from a belief in the dignity of the individual, freedom, and equality not only for Americans but for all people on earth."

- Eleanor Roosevelt, First Lady, and Human Rights Advocate

"The supreme quality for leadership is unquestionably integrity."

- President Dwight D. Eisenhower

"The fate of America cannot depend on any one man. The greatness of America is grounded in principles and not on any single personality."

- President Franklin Roosevelt

"Everyone is entitled to his own opinion, but not to his own facts."

- Senator Daniel Patrick Moynihan

"Whenever the people are well-informed, they can be trusted with their own government."

— Thomas Jefferson

"Knowledge will forever govern ignorance; and a people who mean to be their own governors must arm themselves with the power which knowledge gives."

— President James Madison

"If ever a time should come, when vain and aspiring men shall possess the highest seats in Government, our country will stand in need of its experienced patriots to prevent its ruin."

- Samuel Adams, a Founding Father of the United States

"Where liberty dwells, there is my country."

- Benjamin Franklin, a Founding Father of the United States

"May we never forget our fallen comrades. Freedom isn't free."

- Sgt. Major Bill Paxton, Heroic Bronze Star Marine

"If you look back in history, you will find the core mission of public education in America was to create places of civic virtue for our children and for our society. As education undergoes the rigors of re-examination and the need for reinvention, it is crucial to remember that the key role of public schools is to preserve democracy and, that

193

as battered as we might be, our mission is central to the future of this county."

– Paul D. Houston, Executive Director Emeritus of the American Association of School Administrators

"The essence of America - that which really unites us - is not ethnicity, or nationality or religion - it is an idea - and what an idea it is: That you can come from humble circumstances and do great things."

- Condoleezza Rice, National Security Advisor and Secretary of State

"I received a letter just before I left office from a man. I don't know why he chose to write it, but I'm glad he did. He wrote that you can go to live in France, but you can't become a Frenchman. You can go to live in Germany or Italy, but you can't become a German, or an Italian. He went through Turkey, Greece, Japan and other countries. But he said anyone, from any corner of the world, can come to live in the United States and become an American."

- President Ronald Reagan

"I am an American: free born and free bred, where I acknowledge no man as my superior, except for his own worth, or as my inferior, except for his own demerit."

- President Theodore Roosevelt

"Let every nation know, whether it wishes us well or ill, that we shall pay any price, bear any burden, meet any hardship, support any friend, oppose any foe to assure the survival and the success of liberty."

194

- President John F. Kennedy

"The life of the nation is secure only while the nation is honest, truthful and virtuous."

- Frederick Douglass, Writer, and Civil Rights Leader

"Where you see wrong or inequality or injustice, speak out, because this is your country. This is your democracy. Make it. Protect it. Pass it on."

- Thurgood Marshall, America's First African American Supreme Court Justice

"Duty, honor, country. Those three hallowed words reverently dictate what you ought to be, what you can be, what you will be."

- General Douglas MacArthur

"There is nothing wrong with America that cannot be cured with what is right in America."

- President Bill Clinton

"May we think of freedom not as the right to do as we please, but as the opportunity to do what is right."

- Reverend Peter Marshall, Chaplain of the U.S. Senate

"Injustice anywhere is a threat to justice everywhere. We are caught in an inescapable network of mutuality, tied in a single garment of destiny. Whatever affects one directly, affects all indirectly."

- Martin Luther King, Jr., Iconic Civil Rights Leader

"I have in mind the Founding Fathers' idea of an informed citizenry. This is the basic principle that underlies our national system of education in the first place – that people in a democracy can be entrusted to decide all important matters for themselves because they can deliberate and communicate with one another."

– E.D. Hirsch, Professor, Literary Critic and Author

"The creed of our democracy is that liberty is acquired and kept by men and women who are strong and self-reliant, and possessed of such wisdom as God gives mankind – men and women who are just, and understanding, and generous to others -- men and women who are capable of disciplining themselves. For they are the rulers, and they must rule themselves."

- President Franklin D. Roosevelt

"Democracy cannot endure if ignorance prevails."

- Diane Ravitch, Historian and former U.S. Assistant Secretary of Education

"Violence is the last resort of the incompetent."

- Isaac Asimov, Professor and Author

"Change often seems impossible until it is inevitable. Just as we must own our lives, we must own our country. For, we, the people, are ultimately in control of America's story."

- Valerie Jarrett, Presidential Advisor

"We must reject the idea that every time a law's broken, society is guilty rather than the lawbreaker. It is time to

196

restore the American precept that each individual is accountable for his actions. "

- President Ronald Reagan

"Our attitude towards immigration reflects our faith in the American ideal. We have always believed it possible for men and women who start at the bottom to rise as far as their talent and energy allow. Neither race nor place of birth should affect their chances. "

- Senator Robert F. Kennedy

"The land flourished because it was fed from so many sources - because it was nourished by so many cultures and traditions and peoples.

- President Lyndon B. Johnson

"America was not built on fear. America was built on courage, on imagination, and an unbeatable determination to do the job at hand. "

- President Harry S. Truman

"This nation will remain the land of the free only so long as it is the home of the brave. "

- Elmer David, WW II Director of the United States Office of War Information

"Freedom is never more than one generation away from extinction. We didn't pass it to our children in the bloodstream. It must be fought for, protected, and handed on for them to do the same, or one day, we will spend our sunset years telling our children and our children's

children what it was once like in the United States, where men were free. "

- President Ronald Reagan

"We are one people, all of us pledging allegiance to the stars and stripes, all of us defending the United States of America. "

- President Barack Obama

"I cannot do everything, but I can do something. I must not fail to do the something that I can do. "

- Helen Keller, Educator and Advocate for the Blind and Deaf

"I have witnessed time and again the bravery and valor of soldiers defending a country that they consider their adopted home. They are grateful for the opportunities the United States provides, and we are grateful for their sacrifices. "

- Colin Powell, Chairman of the Joint Chiefs of Staff and Secretary of State

"Never let the fear of striking out keep you from playing the game. "

- Babe Ruth, Record-setting Baseball Player

"In the face of impossible odds, people who love this country can change it. "

- President Barack Obama

"When you get to know a lot of people, you make a great discovery. You find that no one group has a monopoly on looks, brains, goodness, or anything else. It takes all the

people - black and white, Catholic, Jewish and Protestant, recent immigrants and Mayflower descendants - to make up America."

- Judy Garland, Iconic Entertainer

"Failure is simply the opportunity to begin again, this time more intelligently."

- Henry Ford, Pioneering Engineer and Industrialist

"Always remember you have within you the strength, the patience, and the passion to reach for the stars to change the world."

- Harriet Tubman, Abolitionist and Conductor of the Underground Railroad

"Nearly all Americans have ancestors who braved the oceans - liberty-loving risk takers in search of an ideal - the largest voluntary migrations recorded in history... Immigration is not just a link to America's past; it's also a bridge to America's future."

- President George H.W. Bush

"Only a life lived for others is a life worthwhile."

- Albert Einstein, Legendary Physicist and Scientist

"The secret of success is to do the common thing uncommonly well."

- John D. Rockefeller, Industrialist and Philanthropist

"... the educated citizen has an obligation to uphold the law. This is the obligation of every citizen in a free and peaceful society – but the educated citizen has a special

responsibility by the virtue of his greater understanding. For whether he has ever studied history or current events, ethics or civics, the rules of a profession or the tools of a trade, he knows that only a respect for the law makes it possible for free men to dwell together in peace and progress."

- President John F. Kennedy

"Immigrant families have integrated themselves into our communities, establishing deep roots. Whenever they have settled, they have made lasting contributions to the economic vitality and diversity of our communities and our nation. Our economy depends on these hard-working, taxpaying workers. They have assisted America in its economic boom."

- Senator Edward M. Kennedy

"Our children should learn the general framework of their government, and then they should know where they come in contact with the government, where it touches their daily lives, and where their influence is exerted on the government. It must not be a distant thing, someone else's business, but they must see how every cog in the wheel of democracy is important and bears its share of responsibility for the smooth running of the entire machine."

– Eleanor Roosevelt, First Lady, and Human Rights Advocate

"When everything seems to be going against you, remember that the airplane takes off against the wind, not with it."

- Henry Ford, Pioneering Engineer and Industrialist

"Twenty years from now, you will be more disappointed by the things you didn't do than by the ones you did. So, throw off the bowlines, sail away from safe harbor, and catch the trade winds in your sails. Explore. Dream. Discover."

- Mark Twain, Writer, and Humorist

"The only person you are destined to become is the person you decide to be."

- Ralph Waldo Emerson, Poet, Philosopher and Essayist

"Success is the result of preparation, hard work, and learning from failure."

- Colin Powell, Chairman of the Joint Chiefs of Staff and Secretary of State

"Never doubt that a small group of thoughtful, committed citizens can change the world. Indeed, it is the only thing that ever has."

- Margaret Mead, American Cultural Anthropologist

"There is no substitute for hard work."

- Thomas Edison, Prolific American Inventor

"I am who I am today because of the choices I made yesterday."

- Eleanor Roosevelt, First Lady, and Human Rights Advocate

"America's future will be determined by the home and the school. The child becomes largely what he is taught; hence we must watch what we teach, and how we live."

- Jane Addams, Nobel Prize Winner recognized as Founder of the Social Work Profession

"Liberty cannot be preserved without general knowledge among the people."
– President John Adams

"Our Constitution is a remarkable, beautiful gift. But it's really just a piece of parchment. It has no power on its own. We, the people, give it power. We, the people, give it meaning - with our participation, and with the choices that we make and the alliances that we forge."
- President Barack Obama

"Americans never quit. We never surrender. We never hide from history. We make history."
- Senator John McCain

"Ask not what your country can do for you; ask what you can do for your country."
- President John F. Kennedy

Throughout our nation's brief 248 year history, wise voices - those of men and women, young and old, of different ethnicities and races - have spoken to each generation with profound words of discernment, encouragement, and inspiration. We would do well to let their words resonate deep within us so that we, too, may learn from those who have gone before us and be inspired to meet the challenges that we face.

When I look at the current state of our politics, it seems that traditionally liberal and conservative ideologies are no longer able to serve Americans' best interests. What we need now is a transpartisan ideology of common sense that serves the common good of all Americans.

What We Can Do

It is incumbent upon all citizens to become informed about the critical issues facing our nation and our communities. With our rights come responsibilities, not the least of which is making informed choices at the ballot box. To help in this regard, below is a Candidate Evaluation Criteria checklist which you can use to evaluate one politician as compared to another politician campaigning for your vote to hold public office. Assess them yourself and decide which candidate will take a transpartisan common sense approach to bringing integrity to public life and inspiring our citizenry.

Candidate Evaluation Criteria

	Candidate _____'s Position on Integrity and Inspiration in Public Office	Yes/ No
1	Brings a common sense, not an ideological, perspective to public policy issues	
2	Exhibits civility and respect in their public and private affairs	
3	Demonstrates competence in handling the responsibilities of a particular public office	
4	Personifies courage in speaking the truth and challenging unfair or bad practices	
5	Shows compassion in empathizing with the real-life challenges facing citizens	
6	Inspires people to become involved as co-creators of our more perfect union	

The information, data and statistics mentioned came from a wide variety of open sources available over the internet. A debt of gratitude is expressed for the hard work of all those people at so many different private and public sector organizations who spend countless hours collecting and collating data, researching information, verifying facts, and producing reports for public consumption, which profoundly facilitates the creation of an informed citizenry upon which our democracy depends. Among those sources:

BrainyQuote.com
GoodReads.com
CivicEd.org
Wikipedia

Attributions

The information, data and statistics mentioned in this book came from a wide variety of open sources available over the internet. A debt of gratitude is expressed for the hard work of all those people at so many different private and public sector organizations who spend countless hours collecting and collating data, researching information, verifying facts, and producing reports for public consumption. Their work products facilitate the creation of an informed citizenry upon which our democracy depends. This book would not be possible without the public availability of their work products.

Among the organizations whose work products are referenced in this book:

Chapter 1 Embracing Our Rights and Responsibilities

Library of Congress

Sutori.com

ThePublicDiscourse.com

Time Magazine

Journal of Education

TimeToast.com

USscouts.org

Department of Defense

Americorps

The Economist Democracy Index

Wikipedia

Stanford University Center of Comparative Studies

Population Reference Bureau

PewResearch.org

USAfacts.org

ScienceDirect.org

Statista.com

UN.org

Census.gov

OECD.org

Wikipedia

WorldBank.org

Chapter 2 Respecting The Dignity of Workers

Bible

U.S. Department of Labor

Library of Congress

Wikipedia

Time Magazine

Economic Policy Institute

National Archives

Forbes

History Channel

Investopedia.com

OSHA.gov

Britannica.com

IBM.com

SSA.gov

FederalReserveHistory.org

BusinessInsider.com

Chapter 3 Honoring Our Shared Stages of Life

Navigating the Twelve Stages of Life, Thomas Armstrong

Statista.com

USAFacts.org

StrengthenHealthcare.org

Society for Human Resource Management

ScienceDirect.com

U.S. Bureau of Labor Statistics

Chapter 4 Balancing Crime and Punishment

FBI Uniform Crime Reports

U.S. Department of Justice

Bureau of Justice Statistics

UN Office on Drugs and Crime

Google

Wikipedia

PewResearch.org

AmericanActionForum.org

Economist.com

Statista.com

Global Peace Index

NationMaster.com

HealthData.org

Institute for Health Metrics and Evaluation

AmericanProgress.org

USAFacts.org

Chapter 5 Managing Immigration and Border Security

Statista.com

USAFacts.org

U.S. News and World Report

Library of Congress

Census.gov

Wikipedia

WorldAtlas.com

BBC

Britannica.com

PewTrusts.org

CATO.org

ImmigrationEquality.org

WelcomeCorps.org

USVisaNet.com

BusinessPundit.com

NationsOnline.org

Chapter 6 Preserving Public Safety and Gun Rights

EveryTownResearch.org

SandyHookPromise.org

BradyUnited.org

GunPolicy.org

GunViolenceArchive.org

Bureau of Alcohol, Tobacco, Firearms and Explosives

FBI Uniform Crime Reports

U.S. Department of Justice

National Institute of Justice

USAfacts.org

Statista.com

CDC

BBC

NPR

National Safety Council

Injury Epidemiology Journal

Harvard Injury Control Research Center

WorldPopulationReview.com

Office of the United States Surgeon General

Chapter 7 Creating a Culture of Life

ThePublicDiscourse.com

Chapter 8 Pursuing a Foreign Policy of Global Leadership

Wikipedia

Britannica.com

Department of Defense

Foreign Affairs

History.com

History.Army.mil

History.State.gov

HistoryOfWar.org

Library of Congress

Office of the U.S. Trade Representative

OurWorldInData.org

NYTimes.com Best Books of 2023, "What Every Person Should Know About War" by Chris Hedges

The World Bank

The Hill, "Our Unraveling World Is History Repeating Itself" by Robert Manning

Annual Threat Assessment, February 5, 2024, Director of National Intelligence

Chapter 9 Thriving in the Land of Opportunity

Migration Policy Institute

Statista.com

World.Population.Review.com

Wikipedia

"Public and Private Families," Andrew Cherlin (2009)

"Success Stories," Joe Soss (2002)

Center on Budget and Policy Priorities

National Women's Law Center

The New Republic, September 2006

Google

Economist.com

USDA.gov

USAFacts.org

Chapter 10 Ensuring Political Integrity

OpenSecrets.org

U.S. News and World Report

U.S. Department of the Treasury

Economic Policy Institute

Federal Bureau of Investigation

Fiscal Policy Institute

JAMA

Wikipedia

The New York Times

The Wall Street Journal

CivicsRenewalNetwork.org

GoodReads.com

Conclusion

BrainyQuote.com

GoodReads.com

CivicEd.org

Wikipedia

Author

Jerry H. Parisella is an author, semi-retired pension consultant, former talent development professional, previous corporate banker, and a U. S. Air Force veteran. He was born in Washington, DC, grew up in Massachusetts, earned a Bachelors Degree summa cum laude in political science at Gordon College and a Masters Degree in international affairs from the Walsh School of Foreign Service at Georgetown University. He and his wife, Anna, who earned her Bachelors Degree in economics in Kyiv, Ukraine, and later emigrated to the United States, currently make their home in New York City with their rescued sweet Dachshund, Melissa.

Jerry considers himself an average, middle class, middle-of-the road American. He started his career as a corporate banker, managing financial relationships with Fortune 1000 companies. After seventeen years in corporate finance, he made a mid-career change to serve as the U.S. Managing Director of a London-based executive education company. After eight years, he and a business school professor launched their own company, designing onsite and online talent development programs for clients in North America and Europe. After seven years, he returned to the financial space, taking a position as a pension consultant.

While working over four decades, he also variously volunteered in an education outreach program for the homeless, sat on a grants committee to assess the eligibility of non-profit organizations, participated in entertainment programs for seniors, and wrote the book, Stop Eating The Animals. He is of Italian-American and Romanian ancestry. His father, Henry, born in the U.S. to Italian immigrants who came to America in 1900, spent his career working for the U.S. State Department in Washington, DC, and at embassies in Europe. Jerry's mother, Angela, was born in Romania when it was a constitutional monarchy and, as a young bride, fled the

Communist regime in 1948 to make a new life with Henry in the United States, where she later gave birth to Jerry in 1954.

Jerry's family history, foreign travel, military service, exposure to the three main traditions of Christianity, volunteering, large corporate, international, and small business experience, and long professional career have together shaped his political, economic, social, and spiritual views. He has seen how American freedom and opportunity are unrivalled in the world, how oppressive governments deny people their God-given rights, how corrupt governments aggregate power to themselves to the detriment of their citizens, and how failing governments and tribal rivalries deny their resident's basic safety and life's essentials. Each time he returns home from travelling abroad, he asks himself, *"How can we preserve what is good, noble, and works well in the United States?"* And *"How can we resolve the problems that our country faces today so that future generations won't inherit them?"*

His intent in sharing his observations in this book is to contribute to public discourse by drawing attention to certain problematic practices that have crept into contemporary American society and to offer suggestions from a transpartisan common sense perspective. His hope is that we can leverage the diversity of our life experiences and collaborate on common ground to get us closer to that *'more perfect union'* noted in the preamble of the U.S. Constitution.

For more information or to email the author, you are invited to visit the website AmericanCommonSense.org

Candidate Checklists

What We Can Do

It is incumbent upon all citizens to become informed about the critical issues facing our nation and our communities. With our rights come responsibilities, not the least of which is making informed choices at the ballot box.

To help in this regard, on the pages which follow you will find issue-specific candidate evaluation checklists that you can use to evaluate politicians campaigning for your vote to hold public office. Assess them yourself and decide which candidate is best prepared and most likely to take a transpartisan, common sense approach to each of these important public policy areas.

Please note: The last two pages contain a chart of the proposed monthly holidays to honor American workers. Feel free to share them with your colleagues, friends, and relatives, even your elected representatives. Perhaps we can together develop some momentum to honor those who do the heavy lifting in our society with some well deserved additional days of rest and recognition.

Candidate Evaluation Criteria

Embracing Citizen Rights and Responsibilities

	Candidate _____'s Position on Citizen Rights and Responsibilities	Yes/No
1	Advocates adding moral values teaching and critical thinking to high school curricula	
2	Sponsors tuition and tax incentives to encourage public and military service	
3	Strengthens oversight of tech companies to limit harmful content and illegal activity	
4	Creates public service advertising campaigns that teach personal and civic responsibilities	
5	Requires formal orientation of immigrants to expected personal and civic responsibilities	
6	As a public official, models those personal and civic responsibilities.	

Candidate Evaluation Criteria

Respecting the Dignity of Workers

	Candidate _____'s Position on American Workers	Yes/No
1	Supports policies which discourage off-shoring of American jobs	
2	Supports policies which reduce dependence on foreign suppliers	
3	Encourages business to wisely manage automation and use of AI	
4	Encourages strengthening of pension benefits to sustain consumer purchasing power	
5	Advances substantially raising annual income cap for social security contributions	
6	Advances a monthly holiday schedule to honor various categories of workers	

Candidate Evaluation Criteria
Honoring Our Shared Stages of Life

	Candidate _____'s Position on Our Shared Stages of Life	Yes/No
1	Advocates universal citizen access to healthcare through all life stages	
2	Encourages nutrition education in schools and public service messages	
3	Incentivizes grocery stores to invest widely in communities to eliminate food deserts	
4	Provides incentives for talented people to choose careers in healthcare	
5	Advances legislation to fund scientific and preventive medicine research	
6	Encourages citizen responsibility for managing their health and wellbeing	

Candidate Evaluation Criteria

Balancing Crime and Punishment

	Candidate _____'s Position on Crime and Punishment	Yes/No
1	Seeks to unburden our correctional system of drug-only offenders and put them into drug treatment facilities	
2	Advocates separating first time offenders - with a presumed greater likelihood of rehabilitation - from repeat offenders with a demonstrably entrenched criminal mind	
3	Supports incarcerating juvenile offenders in military-style boot camps instead of detention centers	
4	Makes going to prison truly frightening – not by family standards but by street standards - and embed "three strikes and you're out' into sentencing guidelines	
5	Advocates running PSAs that if someone commits the crime, they will do the time, and it will be the most miserable experience of their lives	
6	Supports public work-study programs as work-as-last-resort for those unable to find legitimate jobs on their own	
7	Encourages reform of our criminal defense services to have confidence that each citizen, irrespective of socioeconomic circumstances, can truly get a fair trial	

Candidate Evaluation Criteria

Managing Immigration and Border Security

	Candidate _____'s Position on Immigration and Border Security	Yes/No
1	Will prioritize securing our southern border with adequate personnel and equipment	
2	Will provide adequate resources for rapid adjudication of asylum requests	
3	Will base any immigration reform upon a three-tiered foundation of enhancing our economy, executing our foreign policy, and extending our compassion	
4	Will create American cultural orientation programs and require immigrants' attendance as a condition of asylum	
5	Will provide pathways to citizenship for law-abiding immigrants already in the country and expedited deportation for convicted law-breaking immigrants	
6	Will create for nationwide distribution of public service announcements encouraging mutual respect, civility, and shared common values to enhance community life.	

Candidate Evaluation Criteria

Preserving Public Safety and Gun Rights

	Candidate _____'s Position on Gun Rights and Responsibilities	Yes/No
1	Supports amnesty programs to voluntarily turn in guns without fear of retribution	
2	Would allocate resources for buy back programs to reduce guns in our communities	
3	Would support federal criteria mandated state gun registries and periodic gun relicensing	
4	Would require weapons training and safety inspections of all gun license applicants	
5	Supports a ban on assault weapons, large capacity magazines, and armor piercing bullets	
6	Advocates for severe, swift and sure punishment for illegal weapons possession	

Candidate Evaluation Criteria
Creating a Culture of Life

	Candidate _____'s Position on Creating a Culture of Life	Yes/No
1	Allows women and doctors fully informed healthcare choices without fear of liability	
2	Supports widely advertised and available alternatives to abortion	
3	Encourages age appropriate comprehensive sex education and access to contraception	
4	Favors highly restrictive lifetime imprisonment as an alternative to capital punishment	
5	Supports making inmates work to help compensate for the cost of their incarceration	
6	Funds expanded availability of hospice care and pain medications for the terminally ill	

Candidate Evaluation Criteria

Pursuing a Foreign Policy of Global Leadership

	Candidate _____'s Position on Foreign Policy	Yes/No
1	Has a solid understanding of history and international relations	
2	Supports a strong military with the ability to project power globally	
3	Seeks to advance international relations through robust diplomacy	
4	Endeavors to strengthen and expand alliance relationships like NATO and others	
5	Advances U.S. leadership at the United Nations and at multilateral institutions like the International Monetary Fund and World Bank	
6	Fosters public-private partnerships to advance our foreign policy objectives	
7	Encourages civic education and communication about our foreign policies	

Candidate Evaluation Criteria

Thriving in the Land of Opportunity

	Candidate _____'s Position on Opportunity and Responsibility	Yes/No
1	Supports educational campaigns that encourage work and self-reliance	
2	Advances efforts to improve the eligibility and effectiveness of welfare programs	
3	Tightens enforcement of child support from baby fathers	
4	Works to increase affordability and access to child care	
5	Advocates for education and vocational training to secure better paying jobs	
6	Equips government agencies to prosecute individual and organizational fraud	
7	Supports expanding the teaching of civic responsibilities and laws throughout society	
8	Encourages judging people on behavior and admonishes judging people on appearance	
9	Provides for the teaching of good moral values in our schools, media, and institutions	
10	Sets an example as a public official of making morally sound choices	

Candidate Evaluation Criteria

Ensuring Political Integrity

	Candidate _____'s Position on Campaign Reform, Ethics and Universally Applicable Law	Yes/No
1	Supports a cap on campaign spending based upon district or state demographics to not advantage one candidate over another	
2	Supports a short duration time frame before elections for politicians, political parties, and advocacy groups to campaign and advertise in any medium to reduce the amount of money campaigns need to raise, to have elected officials spend more time governing, and to better focus voters' attention closer to elections	
3	Advocates for closing loopholes on elected officials and appointed officials' acceptance of money, largesse, perquisites, jobs, contracts, etc., from private citizens and organizations before, during, and up to ten years after finishing public service	
4	Advocates for campaign finance reform that transforms organizations and individuals contributing directly to politicians, their campaigns, and their political parties in favor of contributing to a public fund from which monies are disbursed equitably to the political parties for their politicians	

5	Supports full public disclosure, no later than thirty days before an election, of all sources of financial or in kind contributions to any candidate or campaign, the failure of which would disqualify the candidate's appearance on a ballot	
6	Favors strengthening ethics rules and enforcement for all executive, legislative, and judicial branch officials	
7	Advocates for the adoption of recusal requirements and term limits for justices of the U.S. Supreme Court	
8	Supports a constitutional amendment clarifying that presidents don't have immunity from federal criminal indictment, trial, conviction, or sentencing by virtue of having served as president	

My Favorite Quotes, Ideas and Concerns

Why not write down some of your favorite quotes and sources of inspiration? Perhaps this will energize you to pick an issue of concern to you and to champion possible common sense solutions.

	My Favorite Quotes	Why They Inspire Me
	My Concerns	What I Can Do

226

Proposed Monthly Holidays for American Workers

CATEGORY OF WORKERS	MONTHLY HOLIDAYS Dates to be determined	WORKER EXAMPLES
Emergency Services And Law Enforcement	**January** Plus New Year's Day, January 1st M L King Day 3rd Monday	Fire Fighters, EMS Technicians, Police Officers, Dispatchers, District Attorneys, Public Defenders, Judges, Law Clerks, Court Staff, Correctional Officers, Probation Officers
Governance and Public Service	**February** Plus Presidents Day 3rd Monday	FEDERAL: CIA Analysts, CDC Scientists, DOT Regulatory Staff, FAA Investigators STATE: Comptrollers, Health Commissioners, Auditors, Environmental Engineers, Civil Service Staff LOCAL: Town Clerks, Sanitation Workers, Parks Staff, Election Observers

Healthcare	March Aligned with Doctors Day March 30th	Medical Researchers, Doctors, Nurses, Dentists, Hygienists, Technicians, Optometrists, Pharmacists, Respiratory Therapists, Medical Records Keepers, Hospital Custodial Staff, Assisted Living Staff
Personal and Pet Services	April Aligned with World Veterinary Day last Saturday	Hair Dressers, Manicurists, Massage Therapists, Health Club Trainers, Homecare Attendants, House Cleaners, Landscapers, Snow Clearers, Contractors, Veterinarians, Animal Shelter Staff, Adoption Volunteers
Families and Friends	May Plus Memorial Day last Monday	Spouses, Partners, Singletons, Parents, Foster Parents, Grandparents, Children, Grandchildren, Cousins, Aunts, Uncles, Nieces, Nephews, Friends, Neighbors
Agriculture and Food Services	June Plus Emancipation Day Juneteenth June 19th	Farmers, Farm Workers, Equipment Suppliers, Food Inspectors, Lab Technicians, Food Label Makers, Transporters, Chefs, Short Order Cooks, Kitchen Staff, Servers, Bartenders, Baristas

Energy and Telecom	**July** Plus Independence Day July 4th	Energy producers, Power Distributors, Environmental Scientists, Network Managers, Cable Layers, Shippers, Line Workers, Web Developers, Software Writers, Cyber Security Analysts
Retailers	**August**	Product Designers, Merchandise Buyers, Import Managers, Warehouse Workers, Customer Service Representatives, Delivery Services Personnel
Education	**September** Plus Labor Day 1st Monday	Teachers, Administrators, Aides, Tutors, Special Needs Educators, Coaches, Custodians, School Crossing Guards, Speech Pathologists, Translators, Maintenance Staff, Groundskeepers
Construction and Transport	**October** Plus Columbus Day + Indigenous Peoples Day 2nd Monday	Architects, Equipment Operators, Tradesmen and Tradeswomen, Laborers, Pilots, Flight Crews, Aircraft Servicing Staff, Conductors, Track Maintainers, Drivers, Auto Workers, Mechanics
Military and Civilian Service	**November** Plus Veterans Day Nov 11th Thanksgiving 4th Thursday	Veterans, Active Duty Military and Coast Guard, Reservists, Community Activists, Project Organizers, Senior Center Personnel, Homeless Shelter Staff, Food Bank Volunteers, Readers For The Blind

Mental Health and Spiritual Services	**December** Plus December 25th Christmas	Psychiatrists, Psychologists, Therapists, Substance Abuse Counselors, Social Workers, Benefits Case Managers, Priests, Pastors, Rabbis, Imams, Worship Service Videographers, Therapy Animal Healers

Made in United States
North Haven, CT
01 October 2024

58155910R00128